"*The Garden Within* b
connected to the true
abundant life. The au
through the secret place
and with the proper love and care that only the Master can p..
becomes a place bursting with life and beauty."

—ANDREA LOWE,
mobilizer, teacher, friend, fellow traveler

"*The Garden Within* is a beautiful allegory. It has a heartfelt tenderness that will touch your soul. This redemptive story ignited a hope inside of me to find my own redemption story in God. *The Garden Within* will become your story."

—AMY CHRISTINE PROCTOR,
Frontier flight attendant

"*The Garden Within* has powerful revelation and insight into the Master Gardener and His love for His beloved Bride! You will be drawn into a deeper walk with Christ—to know Him and to be known by Him—embark on the journey!"

—CHERRI HOULE,
kindred sister in Christ

"God has given Emma unique insight into tending His most precious possession—your heart. Allow Him to touch and change the garden within you as you see His truths from a different perspective."

—JERRY BIRDSALL,
intercessor, friend, gardener

Who hasn't felt loss—through death, desertion, divorce, carelessness? Who hasn't ever asked, "Why me?" "What did I do wrong?" "What do I do now?" This talented writer has made—is still making—an amazing journey, and she shares her story to help others going through difficult times. Her journey, from loss to recovery, fills these pages with hope and encouragement.

—VAL DUMOND,
author/editor

The Garden Within

A Journey to Wholeness

EMMA KELLN

Copyright © 2013 Emma Kelln.

All rights reserved. No part of this book may be used or reproduced by any means, graphic, electronic, or mechanical, including photocopying, recording, taping or by any information storage retrieval system without the written permission of the publisher except in the case of brief quotations embodied in critical articles and reviews.

WestBow Press books may be ordered through booksellers or by contacting:

WestBow Press
A Division of Thomas Nelson
1663 Liberty Drive
Bloomington, IN 47403
www.westbowpress.com
1-(866) 928-1240

Because of the dynamic nature of the Internet, any web addresses or links contained in this book may have changed since publication and may no longer be valid. The views expressed in this work are solely those of the author and do not necessarily reflect the views of the publisher, and the publisher hereby disclaims any responsibility for them.

Any people depicted in stock imagery provided by Thinkstock are models, and such images are being used for illustrative purposes only.

Certain stock imagery © Thinkstock.

ISBN: 978-1-4497-8929-9 (sc)
ISBN: 978-1-4497-8930-5 (hc)
ISBN: 978-1-4497-8928-2 (e)

Library of Congress Control Number: 2013905259

Printed in the United States of America.

WestBow Press rev. date: 7/31/2013

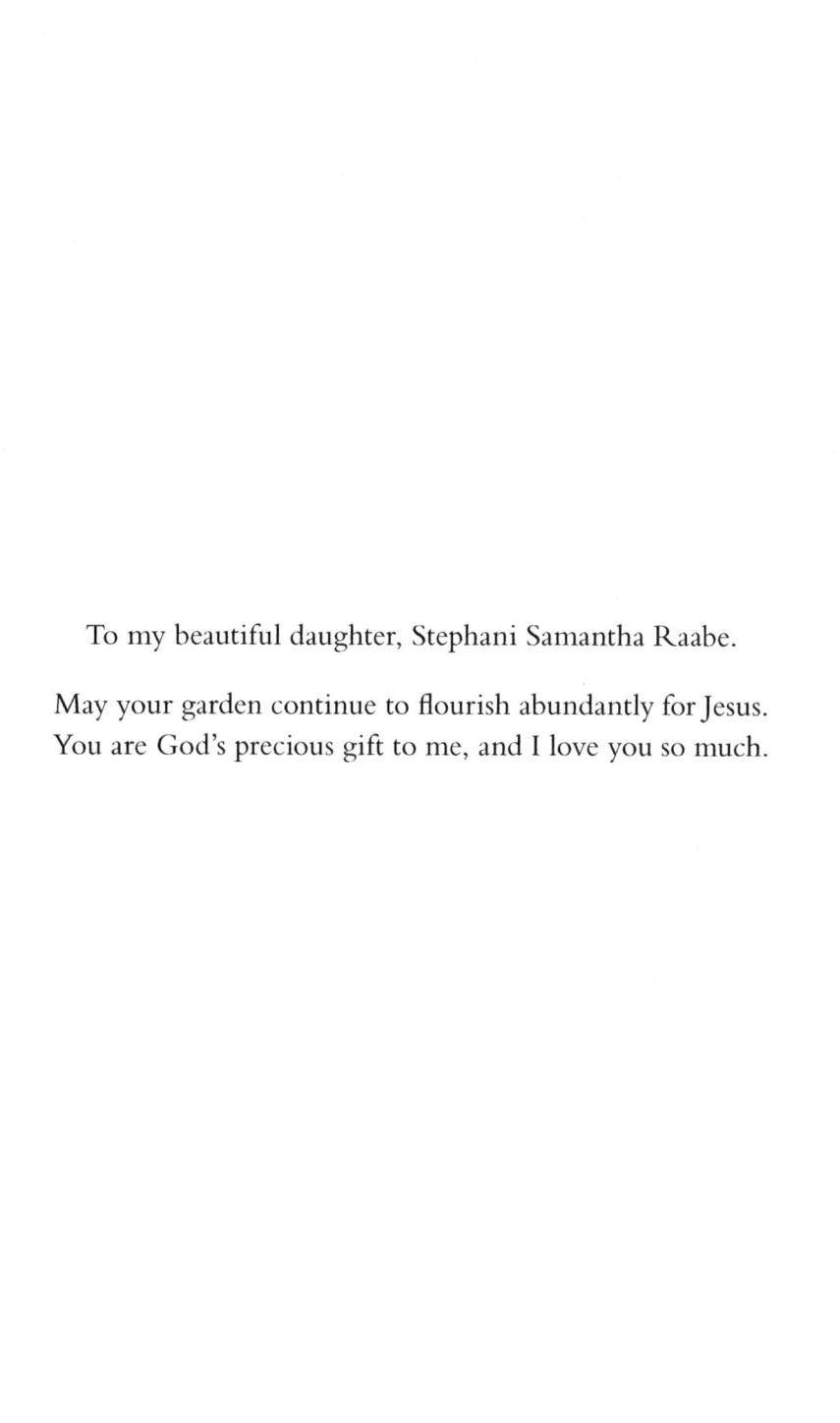

To my beautiful daughter, Stephani Samantha Raabe.

May your garden continue to flourish abundantly for Jesus. You are God's precious gift to me, and I love you so much.

Contents

Foreword . . . . *ix*
Preface . . . .*xiii*
Acknowledgments . . . . *xvii*
Introduction . . . .*xix*
Chapter 1 The Garden 1
Chapter 2 A Secret Process 6
Chapter 3 Awakened 10
Chapter 4 Dark but Comely 18
Chapter 5 Foundation 24
Chapter 6 Purpose 31
Chapter 7 Life 38
Chapter 8 The Vineyard 49
Chapter 9 Come for a Swim 57
Chapter 10 Weeds 64
Chapter 11 Under the Cedar Tree 75
Chapter 12 You Look Just Like Your Dad 84
Chapter 13 I Will Change Your Name 93
Chapter 14 Fruit 99
Chapter 15 Crossing the Jordan 105
Scripture References *115*
Sources *121*

Foreword

It is both a privilege and an honor to introduce you, the reader, to my dear friend Emma Kelln. I have known Emma for seventeen years. When I rededicated my life to the Lord back in 1996, I prayed and asked God to bring into my life godly friendships that were ordained by Him. Emma was one of the first women whom God brought into my life. She influenced me to want to have an intimate relationship with the Lord, and her hunger for the Word made me want that for myself. She is known for her encouraging spirit, and she speaks the truth in love even when it is not an easy thing to do. I am thankful for this friendship, because we all know that life can be hard and people can be hard on each other. Emma has rejoiced with me during the good times and wept with me during the hard times. We all experience dark and difficult times in our lives, and it is encouraging to have others to help you through those difficult times.

The Garden Within: A Journey to Wholeness was birthed out of a difficult season in her life, and I am a personal witness to the awesome work of our Father in heaven in Emma's life.

The Garden Within will change the way you see yourself: you will begin to see yourself the way the Lord sees you. The journey within these pages, walking hand in hand with Jesus through your soul, has the ability to heal your heart and soul of all lies, hurt, and pain, and it will help you live again. It will help you find your purpose in Him.

In Matthew 13:52, the Scripture says that every teacher and interpreter of the sacred writings who has been instructed about and trained for the kingdom of heaven, and has become a disciple, is like a householder who brings forth out of his storehouse treasure that is new and treasure that is old (the fresh as well as the familiar). In this book, Emma brings just this, the fresh and the familiar, and creates a beautiful story of restoration. You will experience intimacy with Jesus in the garden of your own heart. It is the desire of the author for every reader to be touched and changed by God's love, which will in turn bring freedom and wholeness into your life so that you might do the same for others.

You will be encouraged in this story to believe the report of the Lord rather than remain stuck in your unpleasant circumstances. Because of this faith walk, I can now see the Promised Land in my own life. The evidence that someone has had a transformational experience is that they can't keep it to themselves; they must share it with others. It is the author's prayer that you too will be transformed by the power and love of God and therefore share it with others.

As you sit down to read this book, pray that the Master Gardener (who is Jesus in this story) would uproot anything in your heart and life that has not been planted by Him, as in Matthew 15:13, where Jesus answered His disciples, saying, "Every plant which My heavenly Father has not planted will be torn up by the roots."

You can sit and read this book in a short period of time, but I encourage you to take your time and walk with Him through your own garden (in your heart) as you venture through these pages. Remember that God is no respecter of persons; thus, what He does for one, He will do for another.

As for me, I would have despaired if I had not believed that I'd see the goodness of God in the land of the living (Psalm 27:13). I believed, and now I see His life flourishing in my own garden.

Love from the King's daughter,
ABIGAIL FAITH MURRAH

Preface

My heart's desire for you in this journey is for God Himself to touch and heal your soul, your very being, and for Him to mold you into His perfect image. In this process He will reveal to you your restored, flourishing garden (or soul) so that you can then nurture others and help them to grow and be fruitful. In 2 Corinthians 5:17 (The Message) it says: The old life is gone; a new life burgeons. The meaning of burgeon is to send forth new growth as buds or branches, to bloom, and to grow rapidly. Together we can fill the whole earth with the knowledge of God!

The Garden Within journey for me began many years ago. When God took my hand that day, He truly captured my heart. He took all of my insecurities, my hurt, and my pain as He walked and talked with me in the secret place: the garden within my soul. It was there, with Him, that I was healed. The Bible says in 1 Corinthians 3:9, that we are God's garden and vineyard under cultivation. To help you understand the state of my heart or my garden at the beginning of my journey, I need to share with you a very difficult time in my life that began me writing *The Garden Within*. I was a woman that on the outward appearance seemed joyful and doing pretty much okay: but on the inside I was barren, insecure, and had very little of what God calls "the abundant life". I was more like the woman in Isaiah 54 who was forsaken, and grieved, and heartsore or broken hearted, because my now ex-husband had not only had multiple affairs, but had also sexually abused my daughter (his step daughter) from the time she was 8 years old until she was 12. It was after the fact that I found out. (I have since learned that 1 in 3 girls are sexually abused and many never tell. Those statistics are heart wrenching! There are a few great ministries out there to help victims, young and old, and they also teach you how to talk to your children about this violation in our world, here are two of them: Voice Today, Inc., and SpeakingOut against Child Sexual Abuse, Inc.)

After seeking the Lord during this season, there was no fruit of repentance in my ex's life for the great devastation that he caused, and we were divorced. I moved out and the healing began. God Himself took me to the garden within my heart, into my soul, and it was there in the secret place that He took my pain and carried it Himself. He bound up my broken heart for my daughter, although it is still very painful if thought upon, and He promised me there, in the garden, that He would heal her heart also and cause her to flourish, which I have witnessed. For what the enemy meant to harm us and utterly destroy us, God has and will use that very thing to help others to find WHOLENESS and FREEDOM in Him as we share our lives with Him and for Him.

The vision or mission statement God gave me for *The Garden Within* is this: Jesus has taken every hurtful thing in my life and turned it into nourishment. This has caused me to grow into the person He created me to be, to nourish others, and to help them grow.

My prayer is that this journey will do the same for you.

Although this book seems to be written for women, many men have also been blessed by its content. Remember, men are also called the "Bride of Christ."

The Garden Within is an allegory. It refers to the study of elements, such as the earth or, in this case, gardens, as a structure or style used in writing. This one portrays a life change within a soul while one walks with Jesus through it. It is also the art of effective expression and the persuasive use of language that portray communication and discourse. In this writing, the allegorical form is conversations with Jesus in a garden setting. God uses analogies or parables all throughout the Bible about gardens, often likening our lives to one. The allegory style is writing that is movingly expressive.

So I pray that the journey with Jesus in these pages will move you and touch your soul. I pray that the fruit of excellence that comes from walking with Him will become evident in you and in your life and that you will feed the multitudes around you. Most importantly, I pray that you will live your life to release life to others!

Acknowledgments

First and foremost, I want to thank my beloved Jesus for walking with me in this journey to wholeness and for His precious Holy Spirit writing this with me and for me. I am eternally grateful!

I would also like to thank my husband, my next beloved (which is the meaning of my husband's name), Dave. Sometimes I am just amazed by God and how He orchestrates our lives. Thank you for encouraging me in this life as we walk it out together, and thank you for believing in me. You fill my life with laughter and are my joy. I love you so much!

To my typist and friend Amy Christine Proctor, thank you for your gift of typing for me. You are a huge blessing.

To Anselmo Amaro, thanks for your day spent photographing my beautiful granddaughter, Ella. You truly captured my vision for the cover.

To Judy Stachurski, thank you for taking my author picture. You are a gem.

To my Caleb, Abigail Murrah, you have been such an encouragement to me. Like Caleb, you looked into the Promised Land with me in many of our prayer times and said of the giants along the way, "We can take them and take this land back!" Thank you for your many prayers and for your friendship. Huge love!

To Cherri Houle and her family, I am forever grateful for your gift of prophecy and prayer for me in this journey called life. God's words, through you all, truly made me shine for Him. Thank you for your faithfulness.

To my mom, thank you for your poem written for me when I was born. Written from your heart and, I believe, from the heart of our heavenly Father, which said that I would have a love for flowers and trees. The Lord has taught me so much in these two creations of His. I Love you Mama.

To my Aunt Val, thank you from the bottom of my heart for all your help with my book. I am grateful for following in your footsteps in being an author.

To my sons and my daughter, and to the rest of my family and friends, thank you for your prayers, your love, and your encouragement in this journey. You are so very loved and appreciated.

Introduction

You are God's garden and vineyard and field under cultivation.
1 Corinthians 3:9

Here on this ground which is hard now, I will make it a vineyard.
Hosea 2:14-15

Love, Jesus

Are you ready to meet with God in the secret place of your soul? To experience a face-to-face encounter with Him? Are you ready for His heart to meet with yours? Do you have a deep desire to be whole and free? Are you ready to find out your destiny in Him and for Him? Then join me in this journey to: *The Garden Within*, a journey to wholeness!

God, Jesus, the Master Gardener, absolutely knows what you and I were born for, because He created us for that purpose. He is perfecting us to be in His image. Before we were ever born, He knew us! He walked and talked with us in the very same garden you will enter on this journey. Will you let God, the pruner and gardener of your life, fashion you into His very image?

I pray that this book will open up your imagination to the gardener's hand—God Himself working in and tending to the garden within your soul and your heart. I pray that He will give you an accurate description and vivid pictures of the condition of your heart (with and without Him) and the state of the garden that is within you. And I pray He will then release to you insights into your own story and the transformation of that story, scripted by our Master Gardener.

Let's enter in.

Picture this in your mind: a little girl walking in a vast garden setting. There are many walled gardens surrounding her, representing the people in her life that surround her every day. She walks around admiring the beauty in which she is enveloped. So many shades of color fill her eyes in the flourishing flowers that encircle her. The petals display brilliant purples, magnificent blues, bright yellows, and dashing whites, and in the leaves that climb up these garden walls are all the hues of green. Oh, the splendor of this place! She has entered into the setting of this story.

Now picture this: This little girl is you. It is not that you are necessarily young, but she is that precious little child inside each and every one of us: innocent, trusting, and searching. That little girl who longs to dance again, skip, twirl, and be free! She longs to be whole! The woman in this story is named Ally. Join me now as we enter the garden within her as she sees a sparrow fly by as if asking her to follow him. Here is where we begin.

Let our sweet Jesus take you through this story. Take His hand as He leads you through this journey to wholeness.

Here is your story.

Chapter 1

The Garden

Behold, He Comes

Ally was outside in her yard, working in her garden, when she saw a little sparrow fly by as if beckoning her to follow him. She took off her gardening gloves and walked toward her new feathered friend.

"What's over there?" Ally asked.

It was then she found herself before a great garden wall. You could only tell it was a wall because of its massive height. It stood straight up to the sky and reached as far as she could see horizontally. It was one of the most amazing sights she had ever seen. The wall was covered in ivy and decorated with brilliant purple clematis; climbing roses with petals of white, pink, and lavender; and pale, creamy honeysuckle, which seemed to be dancing in her sight.

"It's a garden," chirped the bird.

"Where's the door to get inside?" Ally asked.

It was then He approached her, the most captivating man she had ever seen in her life. He had wavy, shoulder-length hair, and He walked toward her with strength and majesty. The love that came from His eyes as He came near pierced her heart; just looking at His smile, she realized that she was accepted, loved, and adored. She knew in her heart who He was, that this was her beloved, her Jesus.

"I am the door!" He exclaimed.

He is speaking to me, she thought, standing in awe of Him. The words that came from His mouth were sweeter to her than anything she had ever tasted and more aromatic than any fragrance she had ever smelled.

She responded, "Your words are like honey to my soul. I feel them reach into my mind, my heart, and my emotions; they bring such a sweetness to me."

"Your soul," He said, "that's where I am taking you, through this door. I am the door into the garden of your soul."

Ally looked at Him, a bit perplexed.

"You are a garden enclosed, and I call you my promised bride." He held out His hand to her. "Rise up, my love, my fair one, and come away with Me into the secret place, into the garden within you."

"Please," Ally said, "do not look at me, and do not take me in there. I am afraid that I have taken care of and kept other gardens, but my own garden I have not cared for or kept."

He looked deep into her eyes and spoke with more care and compassion than she had ever heard before.

He said, "Before you were ever born, I knew you and cared for you. I walked and talked with you in this very garden, through this door."

The Garden Within

He pointed to Himself, yet she could see the enormous door He was about to push open with His mighty right hand.

"This garden was alive, awake, and flourishing; it was full of Me."

He smiled because He knew her, and He knew He was the author and finisher of her story. He had already seen her garden in its fullest state. He opened the door. They entered, and Ally's heart sank. It looked to be dead.

Oh Lord, it's too late; it's gone, she thought. For all she could see were brown, ugly masses of twisted branches, dead flowers, and fruitless trees. She thought about how her own garden at her home looked after the winter had taken its toll.

He seemed to have read her mind, for the next words that came from His mouth were, "I would know." He seemed to look right through her.

"Know what?" she asked sheepishly.

"I would know if it is dead or alive."

He then took out a small sword and grabbed a little branch that was lying motionless on the ground. When He cut off a sliver of it, Ally gasped. She felt it in her innermost being, because He had actually touched her very soul.

"The wick," He said, with a smile. "Do you see it?" He held the branch out toward her, saying, "It's green! This garden is not dead; it is as alive as you and Me."

Can this really be happening? Ally thought. *Is it possible that it is not too late—that He could still bring change and life to what looks and feels dead and lost?*

He interrupted her thoughts. "It is time, Ally," He said.

She looked up at Him. While gazing deep into His eyes, she saw her own reflection and was taken aback by her love and affection for this man.

As she was being held by His eyes, she repeated, "Time," after realizing she had drifted away in His love for a moment.

"Do you want to stay this way?" He asked.

She held her breath, and He knew her answer.

"Then come away with Me, My beloved, for the winter is past, the rain is over and gone, the flowers appear on the earth, and the time of spring has come. Rise up."

He gently held out His right hand, and Ally took hold. At that moment He grabbed her very heart.

"I'll never, ever let you go," He said tenderly to her soul.

The Healing Begins

She went with Him. They ascended first some rocky steps, going up a hillside, it seemed. Her beloved said to her, "Oh, my Ally, while you are here in the seclusion of these rocks in your garden, in this secret and sheltered place with and in Me, let Me see your face, and let Me hear your voice. For your voice is sweet, and your face is so lovely to Me."

Ally was walking with her head hanging down, ashamed of the mess she had allowed her garden to become. Jesus stopped her, put His hand under her chin, and lifted up her head. They were face-to-face. Her heart was suddenly touched, and she began to fervently sing to Him an old song that she had loved but had forgotten all about because of the difficult circumstances in her life.

She sang, and the song came from deep within. The words weren't just coming from her mouth, but from her heart as she sang with deep emotion and with all of her heart. All she wanted to do at that moment was to worship Him, because there they were, face-to-face in the garden of her soul. He was looking attentively into her eyes and into her soul.

She was loved by God Himself, and at that moment she knew it. At the same time, her thoughts were churning. She had been so consumed with her circumstances that she had ceased worshipping the lover of her soul.

I'm so sorry, Jesus; forgive me, Ally thought. She knew by the look on His face that He heard every one of her thoughts.

Everything around them appeared to be dead, yet Ally felt a little life, a little hope, and a little sun. She glanced at the ground and saw one tiny green shoot coming up; it was only about an inch tall. It was almost covered up with weeds. She bent down and pulled the weeds away from the tiny little plant.

"How did you know to pull the weeds?" Jesus asked.

She replied with a grin, "They were making it so the plant could not breathe."

Life.

He had begun gardening in her soul.

Chapter 2
A Secret Process

There is a time for everything, and a season
for every activity under heaven.
Ecclesiastes 3:1

"This is the secret place," He said softly. "Ally, this is a secret process. Keep what I show you, and what I am doing in you, between you and me for now." He put out his finger toward a branch, and a butterfly gently landed on it. He smiled.

"To everything there is a season and a purpose. There is a time to keep silent and a time to speak. There are a lot of things in your heart and your garden that need My hand, My strength, and My presence to heal. This is your time right now. This is a time for you to heal." As He was speaking, He stepped past an overgrown bush. "There is also a time to plant and a time to pluck up what is planted."

The Garden Within

Her eyes stayed locked on Him.

"Gardens start with planning," He said. "Let Me be the gardener, the planner, the author, and the finisher of My garden, of you."

He was walking along in her garden and looking at every part, pulling dry things off here, throwing aside a stone there. He bent down and lifted up some soil from the ground of her heart. He could not grab hold of very much, because the ground underneath was so hard.

Ally took a deep breath.

He went on, "Do you know what grows in uncultivated, hard ground? Only weeds. Where there is no seed, weeds grow, and weeds choke the life out of things. We will talk about weeds soon enough, though." He winked at her. "It is time, My Ally, to break up your uncultivated ground; this is your part, My beloved."

His eyes penetrated her very being; they seemed to look right into her soul and her emotions. With His eyes He grasped her inner significance, and she felt kept by Him, protected, and covered.

"Will you trust Me, Ally? Will you give up your plan and your heart and trust Me?"

She had been so consumed by her own painful circumstances that her self had begun to reign and had taken her heart captive. In her life Ally was only focusing her attention on the things that were temporal and had no lasting satisfaction to her soul or to her emotions. She did this to try to fill the void in her life and the emptiness she felt deep inside because of past wounds. The things of the world had grasped her gaze and captivated her thought life. She gave more time to them and to the negative happenings around her than to God.

Jesus continued, "Your part is to seek Me, to crave Me with your whole heart, as your soul's first necessity." He stopped and looked at Ally, right into her eyes. "In all the hurt, pain, and troubles of your soul, your mind, and your emotions, I will turn it around and use it all for My good."

Ally thought, *Could it be? Could He really make something out of my life, this mess of a garden that I see in front of me? Could He actually use me for Himself?* She smiled vaguely, just wanting so badly to believe what Jesus was saying to her.

Jesus then picked up a dead branch He had stepped on and broke it in two.

"With what that old serpent, Satan, meant to use to harm you and bring you to total destruction, I will use for good, to magnify Myself in your life and in the life of others. I will use it for the purpose of showcasing you, my trophy of grace. You will show forth My presence and the result of that presence within and around you to all whom you come into contact with by My divine appointments, and you will pour forth my love to the world. I will make Myself known through you to a lost and dying world."

He looked at the ground. "Here on this ground, which is hard now, I will give you vineyards. I will transform the valley of trouble into a door of hope and expectation for you. This garden within you will blossom and send forth shoots, and it will fill the whole world with the fruit of knowing Me, the one true God. What that means is that you will share your story, Ally, and people will come to Me. And you will sing here again, Ally, and you will dance and twirl, as in the days of your youth. You will feed many with the fruits that will grow here, and many gardens will flourish as you walk by them. People will change because of this life in you—because of My life in you."

The sun was setting. The sky turned a rich salmon color, and the night air began to take on a slight chill.

Her beloved Jesus began to sing.

> *I have come into My garden, My promised bride.*
> *You, oh Enemy, and you, distractions of the world,*
> *You can never make My lover disloyal to Me.*
> *She is Mine. Drink, yes, drink abundantly of love,*
> *Oh precious one, for now I know you are Mine.*

He sang this song as a proclamation over her life. With His confident words still thrilling her heart, her beloved Jesus turned, and His physical presence disappeared into the night.

Ally then found herself once again at her little house. She went to sleep that night, but her heart stayed awake; she dreamt that she heard the voice of her beloved.

Chapter 3

Awakened

*"For I know the plans I have for you," declares
the Lord, "plans to prosper you and not to harm
you, plans to give you hope and a future."*
Jeremiah 29:11

ALLY AWOKE HEARING A SONG in her heart. She knew the voice. It was Jesus, and once again He was singing.

*Come away My beloved. Come away My beloved.
Come away My beloved, to our place I'm calling you.
Come away My beloved. Come away My beloved.
Come away My beloved.
I long to be with You.*

The Garden Within

She again entered into the garden of her soul and found that Jesus had been working, even while she was sleeping. She felt a bit brighter as she looked around; things began to turn a little greener right before her very eyes. These words came to Ally's heart: "Yield. Surrender. Give up something. Everything."

"Lord, I want You to be my gardener," she prayed. "Have Your way, and make my soul a beautiful place where You would like to be with me. Direct my paths; direct where I go and when I go there. I just ask that You hold me during this process," she paused for a moment, "and I just want to add that I trust You."

His voice was becoming clearer as she chose to stay in the secret place, her garden. She then felt His arms surrounding her. He had come up from behind and just held her. Her eyes welled up with tears. She felt so safe and so cherished.

"Are you ready?" He asked, continuing to hold her.

She wasn't quite sure what He meant by that, but she responded before her mind could take her away.

"I'm so ready," she replied. "I cannot remain in the state I am in. I heard these words this morning when I awoke and came here to our garden—that I must surrender, yield, give up something, everything. I surrender, Jesus, to Your perfect plan and will for my life."

She took a deep breath and said, "I seek you, Lord, with all that I am and hope to become."

Her words touched His heart. She could feel His very heartbeat because He held her close. She remained so still, and she did not want Him to ever let go. She just listened with her spirit in the silence of the moment, wanting so badly just to feel accepted and loved by Him and to truly receive the great love that He had for her. She began to feel the pain in her heart again from the one in her life who had been unfaithful to her, and had wounded her heart, and made the ground of that same heart very hard and untrusting. Then she turned her focus back to the only One she knew could truly heal that pain.

Jesus whispered in her ear, "Can I keep you?"

She turned and looked Him straight in the eyes. "I am Yours," she replied, smiling, tears running down her hopeful face.

He took His hands and held her face. He would not allow her to look down.

"I love you," He said, looking right into her big brown eyes as she began to weep.

He again spoke, saying, "I love you."

She looked into His eyes and saw her own reflection once again. She thought, *His voice and speech are exceedingly sweet. Yes, He is altogether lovely. The whole of Him delights and is precious. This is my beloved, and this is my friend. Keep speaking, for my heart longs to hear your voice.*

He again spoke, saying, "You are beautiful, My love. Behold, you are beautiful. You have dove's eyes, and dove's eyes can only see right in front of them, as they are focused. Keep your eyes, My love, on me. Look not to the things of this world to satisfy you. Look to Me. Gaze at Me. Only I can satisfy the longing of your heart."

He gently kissed her on her forehead. And they began again to walk in her garden.

Purpose and Planning

"The purpose of a garden is to enrich the quality of life on the land that is under your control," He said. "Is that not why you have your flower and vegetable garden, Ally?"

She nodded, just wanting to soak in every word being spoken by Him. His words spoke right into her heart.

The Garden Within

He continued, "You are My garden, My promised bride. I have come into this garden to give you life and to enrich your quality of life."

He smiled because He knew He was able.

"Your garden can be beautiful by choice, letting Me, the gardener, do My job, or it can remain dead, ugly, and unchanged."

She thought to herself, *You can feel really ugly on the inside even though the outside may look pretty good. Oh, I long to be whole.*

Jesus continued, "My Father always told Me to make use of all the potential land, and you have potential. Why? Because you have the Holy Spirit within you—My Father's very spirit, My very spirit, living inside of you. When you asked Us to come into your life, We came. We came for this land."

He stomped His foot on the ground and said, "There is no such thing as useless land. You are valuable."

Ally found that hard to believe, but His eyes, looking into hers, spoke the truth.

"Now let's see what we have to work with."

He looked over the entire garden of her soul and just smiled.

"The gardener brings the change," He said.

She considered that statement for a moment, thinking, *Does my garden have a choice when I go out to work on it? Does it say, "No, don't take that away!" No, it just yields, surrenders, gives up, and submits.* There were the words again that she had heard that morning. *Oh, help my unyielding heart!*

She looked to Him again, and He was standing tall with confidence. With His vision expanding for her, He continued evaluating the existing plants.

"I plan to keep as many of the better specimens as possible," He said. "Established trees and mature shrubs become important components of the garden—those things that you have been taught by God already, that which is deeply rooted in you. These are established truths within you that have been developed by God—truths that are firm and unchanging, the godly plantings of our Father."

He paused as He watched a hummingbird flutter its wings right in front of Him, as if it were praising Him just for a moment.

Ally smiled.

He continued, "Before any irrevocable decisions are made, existing plants should be evaluated for their potential contributions in your garden."

He kept walking and looking at every little part of her soul. She followed Him ever so closely.

"Contributions of shade and resting places, leaves of healing, flowers in each of the four seasons of the soul, and a place of refuge from the storms of life. And we can't forget the beautiful blooms that give off a sweet smell when the day has been hard and you just need to get away to be with Me."

He turned to a rosebush in her garden, and it immediately produced a beautiful pink rose. He picked it, smelled it Himself, and handed it to Ally. She smiled at Him, and she too smelled its sweetness.

He climbed up a little wall that was built out of unhewn stones and looked over the whole of her.

"Some things that My Father has planted in your life, I will leave as a memorial of God's grace and goodness. Some of them were unpleasant to you, but they will bear fruit that you can feed others with because you have been through them."

He then gazed through Ally's countenance, into her heart. He said, "Those things in your life that crushed you and bruised your heart—I will take those very things and make them into bread to feed the multitudes."

He took her hand, and they began to walk again. A small breeze rustled the trees surrounding them; it was as if they were applauding. He then stopped at a bush that had become very overgrown, taking up so much room in her garden that it had begun to encroach upon the other plantings of the Lord. It had started to overstep the limits of what had belonged to, or was due to, Another.

"This definitely needs to be pruned. Ally, will you allow Me to move, remove, or prune some things in your garden? Things that could hurt you or give too much shade to the plants around them, thus causing them not to grow in the Son?"

Again, Ally trusted Jesus, responding, "I believe that You will do what is best for my life and my garden." She gazed down at her beautiful rose and then back to Him. "Lord, I choose to yield."

He lifted her up and spun her around and laughed. He loved her submissive heart.

He set her down next to a handsome plant, and He spoke again, saying, "No matter how handsome a plant may be, if it is obviously in the wrong place, it should be moved or cut down. I will not hesitate to take out the shrubs or trees that are taking up so much room in your garden that they have begun to cast shadows so that you cannot see or enjoy more desirable plantings of the Lord."

Ally began to think of the things that had begun to take up so much time in her life. They weren't all necessarily bad things—she just gave too much time to them.

Jesus sat on a big stone in her garden and pulled Ally to his side. "Redeem your time, Ally, for the days can be taken over by evil. There is an Enemy in this world that desires to steal your time away and to keep you distracted. You need to choose to set your mind on the things above and to stay balanced. If you don't spend time with the gardener, He can't as effectively work on your garden."

Jesus stood up and walked over to a stately weed that had grown in pride, haughtiness, and self. The weed immediately bowed. "Will you allow me to pull up these things?"

He bent down and grabbed the stately weed at its surface, where it had begun to grow in her.

"These are the strongholds planted in your life by bad choices or circumstances or mind-sets. Can I pull them out to make room for the plantings of the Lord?"

"Yes," she replied. "With Your grace and wisdom, yes."

With her permission, He pulled up the weed. He had an expression of pleasure on His face and continued, saying, "My will is to restore you to your original form. Remember when I told you that before you were ever born I knew you? That I walked and talked with you in this very garden?"

Ally nodded.

Jesus, seeing her, said, "My plan is to return you to that state and that condition. I want to repair and renew your soul. I want to again take possession of you, My garden, My bride, My love. To restore all that was yours and all of the fruits of your field from the day you left the land even until now. I will also restore or replace for you the years that the locust has eaten, and you shall eat here and be satisfied. You shall feed many and praise the name of the Lord your God, who has dealt wondrously with you."

They sat down under an apple tree to rest for a while, and, as Ally looked up through the branches into the sky, she remembered a song. She sang it to herself as He listened with His heart.

The Garden Within

*Like an apple tree among the trees of the wood,
So is my beloved among the sons!
Under His shadow I delight to sit,
And His fruit was sweet to my taste.*

She felt His left hand under her head, and His right hand embraced her. She drifted off to sleep in His incredible peace.

Chapter 4

Dark but Comely

Dark am I, yet lovely to Him.
Song of Solomon 1:5

As Ally slept, she had a dream. In her dream she saw herself before a great crowd of women at a conference, and she was speaking to them with compassion in her voice.

She said to them, "God wants you to lift your faces to Him so that He can give you His life. His desire is to touch and heal your soul, your very being. He longs to mold you into His perfect image. As you continue to look to Him, He will reveal to you your restored, flourishing garden. He wants to bring life to your soul, so that you can then nurture others and help them to grow and be fruitful also."

The Garden Within

She was so filled with Jesus Himself that He radiated out of her being. He began to touch the very desires in the heart of each woman standing before her, she knew this because they all began to weep.

She thought, *Deep within each of us is that longing to be a handmaiden for the Lord—to be filled and changed and to be an instrument of His love and peace to a hurting, challenged world.*

She began to speak to the women again. "He desires intimacy with you, and He told me that." She smiled. "So we are going on a journey to the garden of our souls; we are going to the secret place to be with Him, to spend time with Him, the lover and caretaker of our gardens. We are going to be recreated by the Master Gardener Himself. It is time to rise up and go with Him into this garden. This garden is within your hearts, because when you find God in your own hearts, you find Him everywhere."

Ally awoke from her dream, and she began to cry. She realized that it had reflected what Jesus had done in her own garden already and showed her that the truths He had taught her were for a purpose—and that was for her to teach others. She was alone now, in the garden of her soul.

Ally thought, *Oh, to be beautiful to the Lord, and for Him to touch others through me!* But look at me, she thought, *I am darkened by the things of this world, and some of the choices I have made. How could He ever use someone as dark as I am?*

She fell to the ground with her face in the dirt and cried bitter tears of repentance for her past and for her lack of trust.

She began to ask herself these questions with tear-filled eyes: Does my soul really crave the Master Gardener, even in the presence of the best the world can offer me? Do I have a constant sense of Jesus' presence with me and in me, regardless of what surrounds me? Do I take time to meet my Gardener each day, letting Him tend my soul? And do I take the time to let Him tell me of His love for me? Do I cheer His heart with my interest in Him, or do other things captivate my heart and life? Do I realize that my voice lifted in praise and song is sweet to Him, or do I withhold it?[1]

Ally was conversing with her soul, asking herself these questions, and covering the soil beneath her face with tears. She was realizing who she was without Him and desiring to be transformed into His very image.

It was at that moment she began to hear the wind rustling the leaves above her and felt it blowing all around her. As she lifted her face from the soil, something beautiful happened. The wind seemed to compact right before her eyes. It swirled her tears with the dirt in the puddle before her and then lifted. She felt a soft breeze touch her cheeks as if a feather were brushing them lightly.

A bottle appeared before her, and the tears that were left on her cheeks gently fell into it. Then the wind and the bottle ceased to be. She glanced down at where her tears were mingled with the dirt and saw a shiny, black little stone. She picked it up and placed it close to her heart.

She asked herself, *What could this mean?*

She lifted herself from her knees and turned to see Jesus.

He too had tear-filled eyes, and He told her the meaning of the little black stone. He said, "You are dark but beautiful to Me."

Ally held her breath as He continued, saying, "Even in your weakness I see that your heart truly wants Me, and that is beautiful to Me. I desire your intimacy, your time, and your worship."

He wiped a tear from His face.

The Garden Within

Ally realized He was crying tears for her. He so desired her companionship and her love that it brought His very heart to tears.

She thought, *He is crying for me.*

That thought grabbed her heart and changed it immediately.

He cleared His throat and continued. "The wind was My very Spirit working with your prayers and forming them into this reminder to yourself. This little stone you hold in your hand shall be a memorial for you. It is to remind you of what We have done for you this day—to remind you that though you are dark, you are truly beautiful to Us. That even in your unrefined state and in the process of being remade, We see you as beautiful—'We' meaning My Father, Myself, and the Holy Spirit. We all have unconditional, extravagant love for you."

Ally could not speak; she just received His words into her garden as she tightly grasped the tiny little stone.

"We are going to replant you, Ally. Your desolate land shall be tilled—land that has lain desolate in the sight of all who passed by and said of it, 'This life is unfit for use and without hope.' Those same people shall now say, 'This once desolate land and life have become like the garden of Eden.' Then those around you, those who have known you before and your new acquaintances, shall know that I the Lord have rebuilt the ruined places in your heart. I have replanted that which was desolate. This is what I speak over you, Ally, and I will do it!"

Ally recalled her dream of speaking before thousands of women, knowing it had to be His hand that had even planted this dream inside of her. She still was unable to speak and looked back into His eyes.

He reached into His pocket and pulled out a little black pouch.

He held it out to her and said, "Here, for your stone. Keep it with you as a memorial of the day when the Holy Spirit revealed your beauty in the process."

She took the pouch from His hand, placed the shiny black stone in it, and held it to her heart.

Jesus then threw His head back and laughed. He was so thrilled with her submissive, captivated heart that He grabbed her hand and began to run with her. They ran in her garden to a river that seemed to have appeared almost out of nowhere. It was beautiful and flowing with clean, untainted water. This river was in her, inside of her garden.

He said, "This is our River of Life. We created it to flow in and out of you. In this life-giving river is the promise, and as you cross it you will receive everything you need for life and godliness. This is where the Holy Spirit retrieved the sediment that, combined with your tears, created your first stone of promise."

Ally reached down and put her hand in the life-giving river. As she did, again she felt His life flourishing inside of her. She looked around her garden and began to see wonderful colors appear. It thrilled her to see that He was restoring her heart right before her very eyes as she received the truths coming from His words. She was changed instantly.

"I am amazed by You," she said, smiling at Him.

He kissed her forehead and said, "You will receive a total of twelve stones on this journey. Each will touch your heart in a special way and be a memorial to you, Ally. And when others ask, 'What do these stones mean to you?' you can tell them of the things the Lord's hand has done to replant and restore your life. All the people I orchestrate for you to touch will know that My hand is mighty, and they too will be changed and worship Me forever."

He looked into her eyes.

He said, "Ally, your life and My life *in* you will cause others to want Me and worship Me forever!"

"Recreate me with Your love, Lord," Ally prayed.

Her prayer touched His heart.

Her willingness to be transformed to look like Him to the world ravished His being.

They both began to sing one of Ally's favorites.

Amazing Grace, how sweet the sound
That saved a wretch like me.
I once was lost, but now I'm found,
Was blind, but now I see.[2]

Chapter 5

Foundation

*For no other foundation can anyone lay than that
which is already laid, which is Jesus Christ.*
1 Corinthians 3:11

A FEW DAYS HAD PASSED SINCE Ally had chosen to come into the secret place of her garden. So when she entered, she was a little leery that Jesus would be upset with her. She walked around, looking at the work the Holy Spirit and Jesus had continued in her absence.

She was a little confused and thought, *Why are they still working on my garden? I haven't even taken the time to meet with them.*

She sat down on a rock and took in a deep breath, admiring the beauty that was being formed in and around her. It still looked to be dead in quite a few areas of her soul, though, and a bit crowded in others.

Those must be the places in my life that need the pruning Jesus mentioned, she thought.

She heard laughter from across her garden, so she got up and followed the sound. She came to a place in her garden where all she could see was a large area of dry land with no growth. Dirt. Just dirt. It was then she saw Jesus on the horizon. She walked for what felt like miles through the dirt to meet with Him. The voice of laughter was still resounding through this dry land.

He then saw her coming and ran to her. He lifted her up and spun her around, still laughing.

Ally tried to join with Him but still felt guilty for not spending any time with Him.

"Why are you so happy?" she asked.

As He set her down, He spoke. "Because today is foundation day, Ally," He replied. "And there is no greater joy to Me than My Father's love, which is the foundation for which everything else grows here. It is the day that He is establishing this firm foundation in you."

"But weren't you upset with me for not coming here for a while?" she asked, her countenance full of shame and regret.

Then He spoke a truth to her heart that resounded across the desert land in her and began to loosen the dirt around her. Even beneath her feet she felt the ground was shifting.

He said, "I want to put more revelation and understanding in your life today. I want to imprint on your heart and to establish firmly in your mind that the reality and the strength of your life is not your commitment to Me, but My commitment to you!" He smiled from ear to ear.

He then said, "When you gave your heart to Us, to the Father, to Me, and to the Holy Spirit, We made a commitment to change you into Our very image. And Our continuing in your garden, Our creation of this life in you, is unconditional. It's unconditional of you coming because We know you will come back; it is in you now to come, because We know that nothing else satisfies. We are shaping you by Our unconditional love. We love you because We created you. When you gave Us back your heart, you gave Us back the ability to form you into Our image and to create fruit and life in you."

Ally was amazed at the progress and the life she felt instantly in her as He spoke.

"This soil beneath your feet is the foundation from which everything else grows. This soil is the unconditional love of God, and when you understand and receive the love of God, everything else just grows! God loves you. We love you!"

He grabbed her arms, put them in the waltz position, and began to dance with her—just like Cinderella and her prince. Ally laughed. There, in the desert place, they danced, and His love continued to grow in her heart.

Intimacy

"We love your soul!" He exclaimed. "Intimacy with Me breaks up this hard, uncultivated ground."

He shuffled His feet in the hard ground of her heart. "Move your feet. Do you feel the ground? It is softening as you are here with Me."

Ally shuffled her feet and giggled.

"Do you remember what I said grows in hard, uncultivated ground? Weeds. Where there are no seeds there are weeds. So we need to plant some seeds! Seeds are truth, and truth brings forth life."

He held out His hands toward heaven, and an abundance of seeds started falling from the sky and filled both of His hands to overflowing.

"These seeds need more good soil, because good soil creates strong roots." He threw the seeds in the air. "So let's look at how we can make the soil good."

He sat in the dirt and, pulling Ally down to sit with Him, picked up some dirt and let it drop slowly to the ground. "In a natural garden, if the ground is hard and unfertilized and not watered, growth will stop, and it could eventually die. Cultivating, which is spending time with Me, promotes the growth of the seeds and the existing plants in your garden. Preparing this soil before planting by basking in the unconditional love of our Father is better than trying to get something to grow in bad soil. Remember: His love is the foundation from which everything else grows to its potential for giving out, and it refreshes others for life."

Ally began to get excited. She said, "So, what you are saying is that by seeking You, and by being with You here in the secret place of my garden, being intimate with You here, getting to know You here, and believing that You love me unconditionally—that is the foundation that will make the ground of my heart soft and pliable again and ready for growth?"

Jesus grinned and said, "Yes, that is exactly what I am saying. Your part is to crave Me with all your heart, as your soul's first necessity, because you will crave what you feed yourself the most, and your appetite for Me will grow as you spend time with Me."

Ally thought about that statement for a while. She thought, *When I begin to eat a lot of sugar, I crave more sugar, and when I watch too many movies, I begin to crave them. So if I spend time with Jesus, I will begin to crave Him, and I will begin to have an intense desire for Him.*

She looked to Jesus and said, "Teach me."

They stood up and walked across the dirt-filled meadow, and Jesus said, "One of the ways you prepare your soil, your heart, is to be aware of what you are saying. You need to let no ugly, unattractive, offensive, or dishonest words come from your mouth."

They stopped and He turned her to face Him. "Do not contaminate your soil with polluting words. If the soil gets contaminated, things will not grow in it. You can pollute the soil in your heart by what you speak. Even self-talk, the things you say to yourself, can damage your soil. For example, when you say, 'I'm stupid' or 'I'm so fat' or 'I always drop things,' these words can harm the soil of your heart. Negative language can clog or obstruct the flow of God in your life, Ally. Negative self-talk also entangles like a weed. It tries to kill the life in you, and it affects who you are."

Ally watched Him as He bent down and freed a little petunia that was being choked by a ragweed. The petunia seemed to thank Him with its freely swaying stem. Ally thought about how many times a day she thought or spoke badly to herself, about herself or others. She thought of these things that did not bring or produce life.

Jesus continued, "The discharge of harmful words can create a polluted atmosphere."

"So our words to ourselves and others can change the very atmosphere we live in for the better or the worse?" Ally questioned.

"Yes. Your words can either bring life or death to yourself or those who hear you," He replied.

"Oh Lord, let the words of my mouth and the meditation of my heart be pleasing to You," she pleaded.

Jesus kneeled down, and as He reached His hand towards the dirt, a little white daisy popped through the soil and grew up to meet Him. He picked it and handed it to Ally. "If you plant in the soil of your mind good thoughts and words, the harvest that comes out of it will be amazing to you," He said.

Ally smiled at the tiny daisy, and it seemed to smile back at her.

"Soil," Jesus continued, "is a complex mixture of diverse ingredients containing all the nutrients that sustain life. My job as the gardener of your soul is to keep the soil in the best possible condition for receiving or giving and to replace the nutrients that plants have taken up. This takes spending time with Me."

He took Ally's face into His hands. "I replace love when you give it. Don't be afraid to love."

Her eyes filled with tears, because she knew she was a little afraid to love again.

He of course knew this already and continued, "I replace lies with truth."

She felt His truth beginning to free her that very moment. Jesus again sat in the dirt of Ally's heart and began to make a pile with His hands. She sat down next to Him.

"To make the best use of the soil in your garden, you should know its properties. You need to know what's in it before you can improve it. You must know its deficiencies. What is it lacking? Is it lacking love, patience, kindness, gentleness, joy, or maybe some self-control? Is it void of peace and faith?" He looked to Ally.

Ally inquired, "Oh Lord, what is in my heart? What in here is good? What is lacking? What is hurting or polluting the soil of my heart? What lies are planted there? What truths? What life? Please show me."

"As you spend time with Me, My love will reveal all this to you. You will know in the days ahead what is needed. My precious Holy Spirit will be speaking to you in every situation and in every word spoken from your mouth. If you listen, We will teach you. In every moment, even in the mundane ones, We are there. Talk to Us. We love it when you glance in Our direction. That is worshipping Us, even when you look Our way for only a moment, knowing We are right there with you."

Ally smiled, and every part of her being smiled with her in that moment. She thought, *He loves me. He loves me!*

She then shouted, "You love me!" and jumped into Jesus' arms.

He held her there for a moment, but even when He set her down, she still felt held. Dirt began to fall from the sky.

"What is this?" Ally asked.

"Sometimes more dirt is needed in your garden. His unconditional love is the new dirt, and it is filled with everything you need for life and godliness. It is more foundation. It is more love," Jesus answered.

Ally raised her hands, and the dirt falling from the sky filled them instantly, just as it was filling her heart. When she pulled her dirt-filled hands to herself, she looked into them and saw a little brown stone that looked to have layers. She pulled it out of the dirt and blew on it to get the residue off. *It's so shiny,* she thought.

"This is your foundation stone, Ally," Jesus said as He smiled, "a memorial to you that the foundation from which everything grows is the unconditional love of God."

Ally pulled the little black pouch that contained her first stone out of her pocket and added this second stone to it. She held the pouch close to her chest, took a deep breath, and began that day with a new foundation under her feet.

God loves me!

CHAPTER 6

Purpose

For God so loved the world that He gave His one and only Son, that whoever believes in Him shall not perish but have eternal life.
John 3:16

Above them the clouds began to swirl. Ally and Jesus heard these words from heaven, and they realized quickly that it was their Father's voice.

"I so loved the world, and I so loved you, Ally, that I gave My only Son, that if you believe in, trust in, and cling to Him you will never perish but have everlasting life!"

Ally's heart was touched by His words; she realized that God was saying that her Jesus had taken her place in death so that she would never experience death, and that when she did leave this world, she would take her last breath here and her first breath in eternity. She grasped the reality that He had given His life to her—a life eternal and everlasting.

As Ally and Jesus continued to look to the sky above them, the voice seemed to take on a form. It was the form of a rainbow, but it differed from one in that each color that formed on the bow was made from various gems—rubies, sapphires, different colored diamonds, and emeralds. These precious stones from heaven began to descend and then formed again right over Jesus, and Jesus spoke to Ally.

"Yes, I have loved you with an everlasting love; therefore with loving-kindness have I drawn you and continued My faithfulness to you. I knew you from heaven, Ally, before you were ever born, and again I will build you up, and I will adorn you. And yes, you were an afflicted garden. Your soul had been lashed by the storms that have come into your life, and you were not comforted. But I have come into your soul, and I will build you with these gems surrounding me," He said.

He pointed to the rainbow above His head. "I am building in you a spiritual infrastructure that cannot be destroyed or even shaken by the storms. Too often, Ally, have you constructed your own life on the sinking foundations of lies and false assumptions, and the city you were building without Me involved was poised for collapse. But I am going to build within you walls made up of the precious stones of My solid truths, and you will be able to withstand all the storms of life that come your way."

He grabbed Ally's hands and began to dance with her. "You will dance here with Me always, and I will plant vineyards upon the mountains. In every difficult place in your life, We will plant there! The Father and I, We will grow the fruit in you to be given to others to enjoy and to truly live. You will give out this true life that you have been given, and you will live it out, and many will see it. They will see Me and be saved!"

Ally's breath was taken away by the beauty of the rainbow surrounding Jesus; her heart was ravished by Him and His presence. Then she turned to see some mountains in her garden.

Following her gaze, He said, "These mountains in your garden represent difficulties in your life. They portray the deep anguish you feel in your soul and the damage in your garden because of your past. But that very place is where We want to plant vineyards and where We want to plant Our truths in you."

That pleased Ally's heart. *My Jesus is going to continue growth in me as I choose to stay and abide in Him, and He will use me to give life, His very life, to others,* she thought.

Just then, this life began springing up all around her, and the once dirt-covered meadow turned into a vineyard as she stood in the midst of it. As far as she could see were rows and rows of grapevines that were lush and filled with succulent red grapes. She realized that the physical appearance of Jesus was not present anymore, but she knew completely that He was still in her midst—that He was the life springing up around her.

He was building and planting in her for a purpose. He was restoring her soul.

Then Ally again heard the Father in heaven speak these words: "I *am* the artist of this vineyard, this garden within you. You, Ally, are My workmanship. I am fashioning you for this world to bring Me glory. I am fashioning you to set you as My display, and I will say, 'Look at My daughter. The presence of My Son is being formed in her. Isn't He beautiful in her'?"

Ally was amazed that God was boasting about her and proud of her—and that He saw His son in her. She began to bite her lip.

Then God said, "I sent My son with a purpose for you, Ally—to die on your behalf and actually live your life for you. Your purpose in this life is to *let Him* live His life through you and let Him live *in* you. The way I reach My world now is through you, My believers. Will you be My hand extended, Ally? Will you allow My love to be poured forth through you? Will you walk with Me and for Me? For this is My purpose for you: to form My beautiful Son within you and to form My life in you."

Ally felt so much warmth in her heart and so much adoration for her Jesus.

"That is why He came to the earth. He came to die for you and in place of you so that you could truly live and live forever," God said.

Ally turned to one of the vines forming in her, and she noticed a huge cluster of grapes. She picked one of the grapes from the cluster, and it changed in the palm of her hand into a luscious red ruby. She recognized that this was the third memorial stone, and she instantly knew the meaning of this one. This stone represented Jesus' death on her behalf and the blood He shed was for her so that she could live a life forever with Him and for Him.

She clutched the little stone tightly. Then she pulled the black pouch from her pocket and added the ruby to the existing precious promises of God. She kissed toward heaven, put the pouch back in her pocket, and she continued with her day with His step in her gait.

She realized after this time spent with Him in the secret place of her garden that she had almost forgotten about a previous engagement. She was supposed to meet four of her friends at a nearby coffee shop. These were four friends who had known her for quite some time. They knew her, so to speak, in her weaknesses.

When she arrived at the coffee shop, she saw the four sitting at a quaint little table in the corner. She sat down and began conversing with them. Something in her countenance captivated her small audience. They began noticing and commenting on the attractiveness of her person.

"What is going on with you?" one of them questioned.

"Well," Ally said, "I have met the one whom my soul loves. I have been spending time with Jesus in the secret place."

Of course her friends had heard of Jesus; they knew *of* Him, but they did not *know* Him.

Ally covered her heart with her hands. "He has been showing me that the secret place is within me, and it is in the garden of my soul. There I have been meeting with Him, and He has been healing me and my emotions and restoring me," Ally said.

She patted her heart twice. "You see, He showed me that I am His — that I am His garden and that He is mine, that He really is alive, and that He is alive in me." She smiled. "It has been a really amazing journey with Him," she said, looking at them, right into their eyes. "He has captivated my heart in every way."

Her friends just sat there, amazed at her words, which came from her heart. They were astonished at the transformation that they were seeing in her.

She continued to tell them all of what the Lord had done and said and was continuing to do. They were so interested in the remarkable person whom their friend had championed with such unstinting praise, and they too wanted to know Him.

One friend then said, "Can we too know Him like this? Where is He? For we would seek Him with you."

Another one said, "This is beautiful, and you are beautiful, Ally. I see this new life changing you before our eyes. I think I see Him in your eyes right now."

Ally replied, "The eyes are the gateway to the soul. That is where He is, my Jesus. That is why you can see Him in my eyes."

By this time all of her friends' eyes had welled up with tears.

"Where is He, you ask?" She looked at each of them. "He is here, with us right now. He is in the midst of us. He can live in you also; all you need to do is ask."

Ally smiled and continued to hold her hands to her heart. "Just ask Him in. He will come. His desire is to come. His desire is to restore, heal, and love us back into wholeness so that we can in turn pour out that same love to others."

As she gazed at her friends, they all now had tears streaming down their faces. She heard Jesus speak to her heart.

"These women are the first fruits from your dream. You are awakening their hearts to Me, and they too are for the first time realizing their purpose and their worth in Me and to Me," He said.

Ally then held out her hands to her friends. "Can we pray?" she asked.

They all kind of looked around and then at each other, shrugged their shoulders, and joined their hands with one another.

Ally began to pray, saying, "Oh my Jesus, who dwells in the gardens, my companions have been listening to Your voice through me. Now cause them to hear it for themselves. Come into the gardens of their souls and live. Live in them from this day forward. Allow them to hear You call to them to come away with You and to spend time in the secret place, because that is so imperative in these days. Let them know You as I have come to know You: as their healer and their deliverer, as their high tower where they can seek shelter with You and be safe. Fill them with Yourself now. In Your name, amen."

They all sat quietly in His sweet presence for a while. The coffee shop seemed to have come to a standstill. It was as if they had been lifted into a whole new realm, a totally different place.

Then Ally joyfully found herself in the garden of her soul again. She turned to see Him, Jesus, and she prayed aloud with her friends once again.

"To the One altogether lovely, the Chief among ten thousand, no one else can compare to You. My friends are eager to begin a life of sweet companionship with you! Make haste, my beloved, and come quickly to them, like a gazelle, like a young deer. Take them to Your secret place within themselves, the garden of their souls, and live in them. Make Yourself known in them, I pray."

Ally and her friends just sat for a time in the presence of this newfound life. What was usually just a time of talking in a coffee shop had turned into a life-changing moment for five women. For the One altogether lovely had come to live in each of their hearts. And Ally, well—she was forever changed!

Chapter 7

Life

I have come that they may have life, and have it to the full.

John 10:10

ALLY WAS BEGINNING TO EXPERIENCE Jesus more and more in her daily tasks. He was becoming clearer and more evident in her life. His voice was becoming familiar in her ears. For the first time in her life He was real and alive, and she knew Him. She closed her eyes, and immediately she was in a walled garden. It was her garden; she knew this because it had grown so familiar to her. Yet here now was this beautiful wall. It was constructed from stones that were not cut with human hands. It was an amazing sight. Moss of the brightest green covered its face. The mortar that held these stones together had cracks in it, and little white-faced baby daisies were growing from within the cracks. Bees buzzed around, collecting the nectar from these tiny flowers.

Amazingly Ally wasn't afraid of the bees as she normally would be. When she finished taking in the sight of this great wall around her heart, she realized she was in a part of her garden that was dead. Old, dry chrysanthemums that once had bloomed with beauty lay brown and ugly at her feet. Rose bushes that had once given out their sweet fragrance now lay barren and unattractive before her eyes. She could clearly see that winter had taken its toll in this part of her garden and in this part of her life. She bent down and broke off a piece of dry, brittle stem from a princess bush.

His voice behind her startled her, and she spun around to see Him. His smile steadied her heart, and she shrugged her shoulders while looking around at the deadness in her soul.

"You know," He said, "when the winter passes and it's time for a new garden, the first thing you have to do is pull up the dead plants."

He tossed Ally some pink and lime green polka-dotted gardening gloves. "You know, the old stuff. We need to take out the old, useless patterns of life so that the new life may come."

He slipped on His gloves, and of course they were manlier in appearance than Ally's little polka-dotted ones. Yet He knew she would think the gloves He chose for her were pretty.

Adorable, she thought.

"Ally, picture us trying to plant new life and new flowers without first pulling up the dead things from the past. It wouldn't be very beautiful or attractive to others who pass by, would it?"

She surveyed the ground of her heart, trying to imagine beautiful flowers in the midst of the dead plants. "No, it wouldn't," she responded.

"I want to do a new thing, Ally. I don't want you to consider the things of the past or even remember them." He pulled out a dead hydrangea shrub from the ground of her heart. "I am going to plant in this wilderness and bring water, new life, and new growth. Can you perceive it, Ally? Can you see it?"

He was grinning from ear to ear, because He *could* see it. "All who are in your life will see it. They will know and understand that the hand of the Lord has done this and that I have created this beauty."

Ally was amazed that Jesus could see the finished work in her and that He knew that work would have an effect in others' lives.

"You are going to help me sow, Ally, after we finish pulling these useless, dead things out of your life." He nudged her in a playful manner, motioning for her to start helping.

She pulled on her new pretty polka-dot gardening gloves and began to help Jesus pull up brown masses of the past in her heart. They worked for what seemed like hours, pulling up good-for-nothing rubbish in Ally's life—useless patterns of words spoken to her, by herself or by others, words and thoughts that had killed the beauty within her. Together they pulled up lies that the Enemy had planted.

When they were finished in that particular part of her heart, they stood again in the midst of simple, plain dirt.

"Nothing grows without seed," Jesus said. "If we do not plant something here, we will reap nothing." He pulled a bag of seeds from His shirt pocket. "If you want a new harvest and a new life, you need a new plan and new seeds."

He opened the packet. "If you want new life, you have to throw away your old seed—the way you used to act and the way you used to speak. You need to sow what you haven't sown before."

The Garden Within

He scratched His head before speaking again, first looking over her soul. "Look forward to the new field and garden, Ally. Don't look back on the old, but press forward."

She looked around at her heart. "How do I start, Lord?"

"First," He answered, "don't carry or even bring with you the old seeds. Get rid of them—get rid of all the negative seeds! For whatever you sow, only that is what you will reap. If we plant corn seeds, Ally, it will not come up as wheat. If we plant corn, we will reap corn. Does that make sense?"

Ally nodded; her brow furrowed as she tried to concentrate and take in what He was saying and sowing into her.

"If you want to reap love and affection, you have to sow love and affection. If you want to reap kindness, you'll have to sow some kindness."

He looked over at the wall in her heart and noticed that the sparrow that had first led her to the entrance of her garden had gotten its little claw caught in a crack. He gently helped set it free.

"And," He said, pouring all of the seeds from the packet into His hand, "you need to sow abundantly. If you want to reap abundantly, you need to sow abundantly." He picked one of the seeds from His palm with His other hand and held it up. "If you only sow this one little seed, what will your garden look like, Ally? Will it be inviting to you or to those who pass by you?"

Ally imagined this huge piece of land before her with just one flower blooming in the middle, and she met Jesus' eyes and smiled.

"I would like to plant more, please," she said, and she giggled.

Jesus then took another route, saying, "The opposite is also true. If you sow to the flesh, you will reap from the flesh."

"What do you mean?" Ally questioned.

"Well, you're either in the presence of the Lord, Me," He said, putting His hand to His chest and smiling, "or you're in the presence of the flesh. You don't have to work at being in the flesh, acting or reacting in an ugly, unattractive way. You don't work to plant weeds, do you?"

Ally understood immediately, thinking, *Sometimes leading a disciplined life is hard. I want to react the way I've always reacted. I just need to tell myself and my flesh, "No, you are not going in that direction today!"*

Jesus heard all her thoughts. "Yes, Ally, discipline seems painful, but afterward, it yields a peaceable fruit of righteousness. Yes, fruit! It conforms you to My plan, My thoughts, and My purposes for your life. When you sow to the Spirit and when you sow to Me, you will be changed into a flourishing garden. You will be full of fruit to be shared with others!"

That made Ally's heart jump. She was so excited to be in this journey with Jesus, this journey to wholeness.

Preparing the Soil

"Let's go back to cultivating for a moment." He sat on a log that was in her garden, and she sat down next to Him. "Breaking up hard ground after the winter is hard work."

He grabbed a spade that was leaning against the garden wall and jabbed the dirt by His feet with a resounding thud. "Changing the way you act or react in certain situations is hard on the flesh, and you just don't want to work at it. It's hard to control your thoughts and emotions. It's hard work to control your tongue."

He banged the ground with the spade again. "Just like this hard ground—if you don't plow first and soften the hardened ground by choosing to remain in Me, by spending intimate

The Garden Within

time with Me like we are doing right now, the ground of your heart will remain hard."

Ally reached down and touched the ground of her heart, and her finger didn't even make a dent in the hard dirt.

Jesus said, "Then the roots of your seeds cannot go deep; therefore, the harvest won't be strong." He reached out and turned her face toward Himself. "There will be no fruit."

Ally took a deep breath.

"Conforming is hard," He continued, "and you have to be consistent. You need to keep acting right, doing right, and speaking right. You need to talk to yourself and tell your mind and thoughts, 'No, you are not going there today,' and change direction again."

Ally sat, taking it all in.

"Again, Al," He said, "you need to get the foundation right so that you can grow, and that foundation is receiving God's unconditional love for you. Remember: God's love is the foundation from which everything else grows. That's His grace. You can do this as you spend time with Him, Me, the gardener of your soul."

She smiled at Him because He had shortened her name as she always did with her close friends. He knew that would bless her as He smiled at her.

Jesus stood up and began to break up the hard ground with the spade. Then He hit a rock. "Sometimes you're going along, breaking up hardened ground, and things are going pretty smoothly. Then you hit a rock, which is a situation or circumstance that the Devil, the Enemy of your soul, garden, and life, tries to rock your world with." He continued to pry the rock in her heart with His spade. "He's trying to move you away from where you are going and trying to make you go in a different direction—that of doubt, unbelief, or fear. Or maybe he is trying to get you to take up a familiar habit such as anger, unkindness, or a bad behavior. And you just can't plow over these types of rocks, Ally. They have to be removed, or they could break your tools! Or, better said, they could break your life."

Ally reached down and touched the rock in her garden. "It's so big; it looks immovable," she said, and she looked up at Him.

"It may seem immovable, and it will be very hard work to remove it. It is like a stronghold of doubt or a mind-set that is trying to stay in your life and in your garden, but it has to be moved!"

Ally thought about some of the things that had taken up residence in her thoughts and in her life: too much television, overeating, addictions, anger, her lack of forgiveness, familiar bad attitudes, old mind-sets or labels, and things people had said to her, such as "You'll never amount to anything" or, "What, are you stupid?" *How do I remove these rocks?* she thought.

"Believe the truth instead of the lie," Jesus said.

Again, He knew her so well.

"Believe what I say about you. Speak that! Consistently speak the truth. Out loud. Say it out loud. There is power in that!"

Ally knew that He was there to help her remove every rock in her soul and her heart that didn't belong. His truth would set her free, and together they removed the one she thought was immovable.

His Living Water Brings Life

They then planted the seeds that Jesus had brought to her garden. They dug little trenches together. Then they carefully placed the seeds one by one and covered them with a light layer of soil.

Jesus said, "After planting the seeds, you water. Every day you water, Ally, even if you don't see anything coming up. If you see no results and no change, you water. You may not see anything coming up for days or weeks, but you keep watering, and you keep speaking life."

As He spoke, He grabbed a hose that was siphoning living water from the River of Life that was within Ally and began sprinkling the newly planted seeds.

"After you plant your seeds, you cannot come and dig them up every few days to see if a crop is coming. Just trust Me, Ally. Trust that I am working, even if you don't see anything coming up yet."

Ally thought of a quote she had recently read: "The answer to prayer may be approaching, though we discern not its coming. The seed that lies underground in winter is taking root in order to a spring and harvest, though it appears not above the ground but seems dead and lost."[1]

Life is coming! she thought. *It is—I am sure of it!*

Jesus then proclaimed this over her: "I am giving you a new heart. I am putting My very Spirit within you, and I will take the stony, unnaturally hardened heart out of your flesh and will give to you a heart of flesh. This heart will be sensitive and responsive to My touch."

Ally clutched her chest, and closed her eyes. "Plant in me, Jesus," she pleaded. "Plant the soil in my heart and mind full of good seeds so that the crop and the fruit that comes forth will be nourishing to myself and to others and life giving."

Jesus set down the hose and embraced her, and they stood in the silence of the moment. She knew her garden had new seeds and life that very second.

The Wall

"You are My walled garden," Jesus said, breaking the silence.

Ally again looked to the daisy-covered stone wall.

"Yours is a garden enclosed," He began, resting His hand on the stone wall, "and this wall is to guard and protect you. Keep and guard your heart and your garden, Ally, for from it come the issues of life."

What are my issues? Ally thought. *If I don't like the way I am acting, I need to guard what I am planting or allowing others to plant in me. How do I plant?*

Jesus so loved her thought process. "You plant by speaking right things. Every word spoken is seed. Who is planting in your life, Ally? You need to be cautious of bad seed and of what others may be planting within you. Is what they speak to you truth? Do their words build you up and motivate you? Or do they tear you down and discourage and destroy you? If they speak or plant lies in you, take those words immediately to Me, and I will replace them with My truth. Dig them out before they take root and grow in your heart. You need to take every thought captive, Ally, and guard your heart. Weigh every word spoken to you, or even by you, because the root source of your words is your thoughts. Don't let bad seeds take root. Don't even give them a chance. If you say something negative, say the opposite right away. Stop immediately, and ask the Holy Spirit, 'Is this good seed or bad seed? Will it bring life or death?'"

He then placed His hand on Ally's cheek. "If it's death and hurt, pray this: 'May every plant which my heavenly Father has not planted be torn up by the roots!' I ask you this, Ally:

The Garden Within

Who are you going to allow to plant in your garden? God? The Devil? The world?"

Jesus looked up into the heavens as if He were getting more wisdom poured into Him. He began watering again and said, "See yourself as a walled garden, and protect it. Guard your garden. Supervise all entries and exits, everything that comes in and goes out of your heart or your mouth. For out of the abundance of the heart, your mouth will speak."

Ally put her hand over her mouth, thinking, *He speaks, and truth floods my soul.* She thought about the many times she had let the world dictate her life. The world would issue orders, and she'd just comply. She removed her hand from her mouth.

"I am not going to let the Devil or the world and its ways dictate my life anymore!" she said with authority in her voice.

Jesus stopped watering and looked at her. He knew that she was understanding, and that this truth would set her free.

Ally said, "I am seeing that what I take into my heart, I will harvest." She began to tear up. "I have let negativity, worry, insecurity, and fear into my heart and have seen them come up, and even out of me. I want You to dictate my life, Lord. I am ready to sow good things with You and to think on what is pure, holy, and right. I am going to change the seeds I have been planting, and I refuse to be the victim of bad seeds any longer. I am going to guard my eyes and what I look at. I am going to guard my ears, what I hear, and to whom I listen. And last, but definitely not least, I am determined to guard my mouth and what I say. I will speak life to myself and others."

Jesus stepped toward her, dropped the hose, and grabbed her face. He then spoke to her soul, saying, "Your field will change because your seeds have changed. Your garden will change because your seeds have changed. Your life will change because your seeds have changed."

With those words spoken, He took her hand and dropped a seed the shape of a large thorn into her palm. "Life," He said.

Ally looked at the thorn-shaped seed and remembered all He'd done for her when He took the crown of thorns upon His head and died in her place. He had begun to walk away from her in her garden, and again she heard Him from a distance.

"I gave you life," He said.

She looked into her hand at the seed, and it had turned into a beautiful green stone. "Life," she said as she dropped it into her black little pouch with the others.

Chapter 8

The Vineyard

God has a purpose in view. Often we shrink from the purging and pruning, forgetting the Gardener knows, that the deeper the cutting and paring, the richer the luster that grows.
Streams in the Desert[1]

THAT EVENING, ALLY WAS IN her home. She had just finished wiping the counters after her meal, and she set her favorite crystal vase filled with pink Gerbera daisies back in the middle of her counter. She looked around her small kitchen and smiled as she prayed, "I am so thankful, Lord. I can even see You here, in my kitchen, in the natural, mundane things I do every day."

She just felt His great peace surrounding her every thought and every move. She ventured into the family room and plopped herself down into her big leather chair that almost seemed to swallow her up. She covered herself with an afghan throw that her mother had made, and she flipped the switch next to her, lighting up the great fireplace. Ally grabbed her Bible, closed her eyes, and prayed.

"Teacher," she began, "teach me." Immediately she flipped through her Bible, and it fell open to John 15. As she read about Jesus being the true vine and how He spoke of His Father as the vinedresser, Ally found herself in the garden of her heart once again.

This particular part of her garden seemed to be very full, even crowded. There seemed to be no more room for growth. Bushes were overgrown and had no definite shape to them. She could see a tiny part of a path; it was overgrown with wild vines that had left their original form and now grew wherever they desired. *No order,* she thought. She was beginning to feel suffocated.

She looked up. "What is this about, Lord?" she asked.

As she looked back down, Jesus stood in front of her with a huge pair of pruning shears. They had wooden handles that looked to be a bit antique and weathered, and then, of course, there were the sharp blades of the shears. She smiled weakly at Him as she thought about Him asking her this question when He first came into her garden: *"Will you allow me to move, remove, or prune some things in your garden, Ally? Things that could hurt you or give too much shade to the plants around you, thus causing them not to grow in the Son?"*

She then realized it was pruning time.

He first walked up to a plant that, to Ally, hadn't seemed that out of shape or overgrown.

Jesus knew her thoughts and responded, "You have to cut back some plants that come up in the spring, and although it sometimes looks worse afterward, it will turn into a beautiful bush." Jesus took the pruning shears and placed them on a branch of the plant.

Ally quickly grabbed His arm. "But Jesus, you are going to cut off the only green on this plant! What will be left?"

"Ally, you need to trust Me." He assured her that He knew what He was doing in her, saying, "We have to cut this to bring the nutrients from the soil; so that they will flow to the other parts of the plant, making it stronger and more beautiful than before." He then snapped the only green Ally could see off of the little bush before her.

Ally gasped and squinted her eyes as it snapped.

"A sharp pruning creates My growth and life in you." He smiled over His shoulder at Ally, who looked a little shocked.

"Think about pruning a tree," He said, stepping toward a tree in her heart. He then looked up through the branches. "We need to climb up there and get rid of the clutter and the dead branches so that the light can reach into it. Sometimes our lives are filled with so much stuff that light, or truth, if you will, cannot penetrate and help us grow."

She loved that He brought Himself to her level with the words *our lives* and *us*. She knew He was right here with her in the process, being Himself formed within her.

"Will you allow Me, your gardener, to have My way with you so that I can prune and shape you into the woman I created you to be?"

"Cut away, Lord!" Ally grabbed the back of her neck. "Have Your way and prune me and shape me into Your perfected image. Do this so that You can use my life for Your purposes. When others see me, I want them to know that You have shaped me for Yourself, and that You have fashioned me for Your use. Create in me Your life, and use me to reach out to a hurting and dying world."

He continued to cut things off the tree within her. He cut things like insecurity and negativity. He cut off the things that humankind had come up with to add to His message, making it a yoke to enslave instead of the freedom that He intended it to give. He also cut off different lies that she had believed.

It almost looks like this is fun for Him, Ally thought.

Jesus laughed out loud. He said, "I see the finished, flourishing garden, Ally. Do not fear. I do have a plan in this pruning."

He continued to cut—and she felt bitterness fall from her. She felt her unforgiving nature break and fall completely off a memorial plant.

She thought about the fact that He had chosen to leave this plant in her garden to prove that He could turn all things to good for those who love Him, even the hard things that came into her life—that He could use that very thing for Himself so that the world may become whole and healed. By His hand He was perfecting everything that concerned her.

He spoke as He continued to cut on this particular memorial plant. "Again, this was unpleasant to you, but it will bear fruit that you can feed others with, because you have been through it. These are suckers, and if you leave them, they will never bear fruit—they steal energy and nutrients from other parts of the tree." He confirmed her whole thought process.

"I love you, Lord," Ally proclaimed.

Jesus touched Ally's cheek as He walked past her to a cherry tree.

Oh, the love that comes from this man pierces my heart with one single gaze. I am captivated, she thought.

"We have to cut away branches that have died," Jesus said, and He grunted as the pruning shears came together and a dead branch came crashing down. "Get them out of your garden.

The Garden Within

Let's cut off all that is not producing fruit and all dead things." He threw aside one of the branches He had just cut.

Ally could see the pile of branches and dead things He was building in her. *Keep going. I just feel lighter,* she thought. Her eyes glistened as she looked back to the lover of her soul.

"It takes severe pruning sometimes to bring forth the fruit."

Ally was amazed at the progress Jesus was making in her. He again knew her thoughts.

"It is because you are choosing to stay here with Me, Ally. That is why you can see the progress. As you spend intimate time with Me, I can work on you. Without you abiding in Me here, I could not advance in you like I am."

Amazing, she thought. *Intimate time in the secret place brings ultimate change, not for myself only, but for others also.*

"As you choose to spend time with Me, we will tend to your garden together," He said as He continued to work.

She could see He was working up a sweat.

"It is all so that others may partake of My fruit and therefore become healed and whole themselves."

Ally was finally getting it. "So You will use where the Enemy tried to destroy me. You will teach me and heal me, and as I learn from You, I will pour into others' gardens that fertilizer to help them grow?"

Jesus knew she was coming to understand the process.

She said, "God has truly caused me to be fruitful in the land of my affliction, that I may feed others through what I've been through."

Jesus could see the tender compassion growing in Ally's heart for others who had walked a hard road. Tender compassion was being birthed in her soul; it was His very heart being formed in her.

Ally looked up through the branches of her well-pruned cherry tree. "Now I can see the light through the branches."

Truth was manifesting in her soul.

Jesus then walked over to a chrysanthemum plant. It had bloomed at one time already, but now all that remained were dead flowers. "If we take off the dead flowers and leaves, Ally, the nutrients of the plant will go to the new buds that are coming. Otherwise, the dead flowers are sucking up the nutrients, trying to live again. Take off the old, useless patterns in your life that have no life in them anyway so that new life may come in their place."

Before Ally's eyes, new mums suddenly budded and bloomed, almost like one of the time-lapse videos she had watched on television.

"There is no time to waste, Ally. Teach what you do know already. Feed with the fruit I am forming in you. Trust Me. I am with you." Jesus then approached her until they were face-to-face.

"All authority in heaven and on earth has been given to Me. Go, then, with Me, and give what you've been given. Teach all that you have been taught, and encourage those you teach to do the same. I am with you all your days. I am with you always, and I continue with you without interruption. Believe that, Ally, on every occasion I am with you. We are one now. Abide in Me, and I will abide in you always."

Ally was overwhelmed with the great commission Jesus had bestowed upon her. She realized that this life was not just about her and that there was a bigger and more majestic picture. Jesus wanted no soul she knew to perish but wanted all to know Him as she did. Now she knew she had work to do: to plant and live His life, to restore with and for Him, to speak, to go.

The Garden Within

Jesus smiled at her with tears in His eyes. She was receiving His very heart into her own. He began to sing, and His voice was sweet to Ally's ears.

> *I am in My vineyard, My vineyard beloved and lovely.*
> *I the Lord am its Keeper, this vineyard beloved and lovely.*
> *I water it every moment. Lest anyone harm it,*
> *I guard and I keep it night and day.*
> *Take root, My garden. Take root,*
> *My vineyard. Blossom for Me.*
> *Open up for Me.*
> *Take root, My garden. Send forth your shoots.*
> *Fill the whole world with fruit,*
> *the fruit of knowing Me,*
> *The one true God who watches over you.*
> *You are My beloved.*
> *You are My vineyard. You are My garden.*
> *You are My bride.*

His song came to her as her life's new song.

It's all about Him now—about Him and for Him, she thought.

Ally was beginning to see His life forming in her, even though she had a ways to go on this journey. She looked toward the pile of branches that Jesus had cut out of her life, and amazingly before her eyes they burst into flames!

She remembered reading in her Bible, in John 15, about branches being thrown into the fire and burned—all dead and useless things burned. They burned up very quickly, and there she was, standing in front of a pile of ashes. She felt the need to dig in them, and as she did, there in the center of them was an ordinary, brown stone. As she continued to look at it, it began to look different; there were little gold specks shining out of it.

Jesus spoke to her soul. "The gardener brings the change. You just have to look for it, and, better yet, expect it. I will bring beauty out of the ashes," He said.

She added the rock to the rest, and then she closed her eyes and prayed. "God, I understand that the most important thing I can do as you prune me is to yield to You. I am done with the things in my life that keep me unfruitful. I am finished being my own gardener of my soul, and so I give You the shears. You know what is best for me. Here," she said, grabbing the shears that were now lying close by and held them up to Jesus. "Please do what You need to do. I want Your Holy Spirit to flow through me in all that I do and say. And I ask you to put Your desires into my heart. I want Your very heart to beat inside of mine. I want the heart of our Father. Let the fruit that is produced in my garden be an extension of You and Your love. I pray that Your peace, goodness, and faithfulness would be fashioned in me. Let Your gentleness be evident in me and Your fruit of self-control be noticeable in my life. Jesus, I need you. Without You and apart from You, there is no life. You are the vine, and I am the branch. Be my Master Gardener. In Jesus' name, amen."

Ally opened her eyes to find herself once again in her big leather chair, the fire before her flickering. It seemed as if the fire itself was smiling and delighted by her.

Oh, the presence of God. There is none like You.

Chapter 9

Come for a Swim

He who believes in Me, who cleaves to and trusts in and relies on Me, as the Scripture has said, from His innermost being shall flow continuously springs and rivers of living water.
John 7:38

THE NEXT DAY ALLY WAS out deadheading flowers in her garden at home. She was trying to remember everything that Jesus had taught her the day before. She remembered a Scripture she had recently read that said that the Holy Spirit, the very Spirit of Jesus Himself, would remind her and bring to her remembrance everything that Jesus had told her.

"Holy Spirit, come" were the next words out of her mouth. She then heard Jesus' sweet voice.

"Come for a swim," He said.

Ally went over to a wooden bench in her yard and sat down. She looked up toward heaven, and she began to hear the sound of rushing water. Before she knew it, she was beholding a great waterfall and the clear and sparkling river below it. She was before the river in her garden.

"This is the living water that waters your garden!" Jesus yelled down from the top of this great waterfall in Ally's garden.

She smiled up at Him.

"It comes from Eden to water your garden!" He shouted to her as He began His descent to meet with her.

How quickly He could move down this mountain, she thought. *Behold, He comes, leaping upon the mountains, bounding over the hills, to meet with me. Oh heart, do not come out of my chest, for I feel you may burst with love for this man!*

Before she was aware of what was happening, Jesus had captured her heart with His amazing love and dove with her into the deep. Her body was submerged in the living water. Instead of being terrified by the deep water, she felt a sense of being completely covered in Him and kept by Him. She knew that He had grasped her heart and that He would not let her drown. Amazingly, she could still breathe. She felt a deep yearning just to stay under this water, for in it she was being filled with the very Spirit of God. Life. This was the River of Life itself. Life was filling every abandoned hole in her life. Every hurt, every lie, and every bit of hopelessness was being filled with this living water. This water was alive.

As they surfaced, Jesus laughed. He loved to wash His beloved ones with the Water of Life. He knew the Holy Spirit had filled Ally with God's very life. He turned to her, and with His hands He brushed her hair out of her face and wiped the water off her cheeks.

"For whoever believes in Me, who cleaves to, trusts in, and relies in Me from His innermost being as the Scripture has said, shall flow continuously springs and rivers of living water, just like this." He was speaking here of the Spirit of God filling her.

"With much joy you will draw water from this river, Ally. This life, this salvation from the Holy Spirit, of which this water is a symbol of—you need to draw it up out of yourself to water both yourself and others with it."

Jesus cupped His hands and pulled some water up with them, letting it fall slowly back into the river.

"You see, Ally, without water you would die. You need to water daily with the water of the Word. Don't waste your time watering with the world. If you take the *l* out of *world*, it becomes *Word*. Cut off the *l*, the lusts of the flesh, the lusts of the eyes, laziness, and lies. Those things bring a life-threatening drought to your garden. Lies are a false statement or belief deliberately presented as being true, and if you don't have the truth in you, you will begin to believe those lies. Wash yourself daily with truth, My truth. Take a swim daily in life and in this river. Submerge yourself in Me. I have ransomed you, Ally, and redeemed you from the Enemy of your soul. Your life is now going to be like a well-watered garden: full of beauty and fullness, bearing much fruit, life giving, and nourishing. But you need to water. You need to spend time tending the garden of your soul."

Why would I want to be anywhere else? I am loved completely here, she thought.

"Praise and worship also effectively water the seeds that you plant and your existing plants." He wrung the water from his hair. "I want to enjoy you. Do you know that is why you were created? For My pleasure. I delight in you, and I love you tremendously."

As He spoke those words, He playfully dunked Ally in the water and then joyfully laughed, pulling her up onto the riverbank. He continued to captivate her heart as He spoke, saying, "When the world comes in and tries to take My place in your heart, keep your confidence and hope in Me. For if you do this, you will be like a tree planted by this living water, that spreads its roots by this river. You shall not fear when heat comes, but your leaves will stay green. You will not be anxious and full of care in the year of drought, nor will you cease yielding fruit."

Ally looked around and saw many trees planted by the river.

"Soak yourself in Me, Ally, because mere surface sprinkling encourages shallow roots, which are vulnerable to scorching in the hot sun. When circumstances and storms in life come up, plants can just die because they are not rooted deep enough." He pulled a wilted plant from the soil in her heart, and its root was only an inch long.

"My love is enough. I am love. I am your *enough*." He reached down and moved His hand against the current of the river, saying, "This water is my Spirit, and He will teach you all things, and you will be filled and give this life-giving water to others. I will water you every moment, and I promise you that if you water others, you yourself will be watered."

Ally had not spoken in all this time; she was just trying to take it all in—to let it soak in, so to speak. "I so want to let You flow out of me continuously, but I feel like I just don't know enough yet," she said, hanging her head.

Immediately, Jesus lifted her chin up with His right hand. "You see, that is the biggest lie in My family right now. You

The Garden Within

need to meditate on what you do know! Pour out your life and the water you do have on others. Give them a taste of the living water you do have, and you will realize that it continues to flow out of you in fullness. You see, it has nothing to do with you and everything to do with Me."

He pointed to Ally's heart. "I live here in you, and I *am* that fullness."

Ally thought, *Truth. He speaks the truth that sets me free.*

"The Enemy of your soul will try to stop the flow of My Spirit in you by filling you with dirt, which is those lies. The world or your own thoughts will try to stop up your well of living water. But don't stop digging it out. Seek truth, and seek Me. I am your salvation, and I will save you from the world. You see, I have already overcome it, so be of good cheer," He said with a smile. "But again, you have to choose—choose to dig until you find water, for My springs are always there. Then with joy you will draw My water out of your life to give life wherever you go."

They stood together, and as they turned, a three-tiered fountain appeared in the midst of her garden. This fountain was larger and more glorious than any fountain she had ever seen before. It had intricate designs carved into it of almond flowers, grape vines, birds, and fruit.

Just beautiful. Astonishing, she thought.

Jesus said, "This is the fountain of skillful and godly wisdom, and it flows like a gushing stream. Its waters are sparkling, fresh, pure, and life giving. It is here for you, in you."

Ally put her hand into the stream of water as it poured from one tier to another. "I want people to drink of You when they are around me."

"They will, if you draw Me out. I will be that life-giving drink to them as you stir Me up within yourself. You shall be like the pool of Bethesda to the world. Just as the one was healed as My Spirit stirred the waters of that pool, I will stir you to bring life-giving water wherever you go, to bring Me wherever you go. Life will flourish wherever this water flows."

Ally remembered the story in the Bible of the man healed in a pool, and the place was called Bethesda.

"This living water is the Holy Spirit flowing out of you continuously, as the Scripture has said. That is My heart for you, Ally. Draw deep into this water. Give My life-drink to those around you, because once they drink of Me, their thirst for the things of the world will diminish. Their wilderness and dry land will be glad and watered, and they will live again. With joy, Ally, give this water out."

Jesus cupped his hands under the flowing water until they were filled and drank from the water in His hands. "Some of my chosen ones are in the desert right now where there is no water, and without water they will die. The waters that I want to have flow through them are dormant and inactive. Those waters in them are latent, but they are capable of being active. They are in a relatively inactive condition, and because of that, some of my processes that I have planned for them are slowed down or even suspended."

Ally thought of Old Faithful, the geyser at Yellowstone Park, and the fact that its period of activity was spaced far apart. She realized that the Lord's plan was for everyone to flow continuously.

She again saw a tear making its way down Jesus' face.

"Will you be My oasis, Ally? In their desert? Will you be a presence of water, My water?"

"What exactly is an oasis?" she asked.

The Garden Within

"An oasis is a small place preserved from surrounding unpleasantness. It is a green area in the desert. It is a place that provides refuge and relief," He answered.

Ally began to realize that this was part of her destiny in Him—to be this place or oasis for others.

"So many of Mine are in that place and surrounded by unpleasantness. I long to give them a drink, to take them for a swim in My life, My river, like I did with you." He wiped His tear. "If they would just come to Me. Will you bring Me to them, Ally? Will you go? Only My water will refresh, support, and strengthen their souls."

With that said, Ally suddenly found herself in a boat on a pond inside her soul, in her garden. She was just lying in the boat with her arms over the side, playfully running them through the water. *What peace and what life,* she thought.

She glanced at her reflection in the water, and suddenly the face of Jesus filled the pond. It was then she saw them coming; for miles she could see people coming to the waters.

"They are coming for Me," Ally heard from within. "Give them a drink."

Ally cupped her hands and lifted some of the water from the pond. The water looked alive because it was moving in her palm. It then took the form of her next stone—blue, brilliant, life-giving water. She looked up at the multitudes and just smiled; she knew she had life within her—His life, for them.

Chapter 10

Weeds

Exuberant and passionate thinking. This is the glorious life of the mind enlisted in the service of God.

"I'll transform her dead ground into Eden, her moonscape into the garden of God, a place filled with exuberance and laughter, thankful voices and melodic songs."
Isaiah 51:3 The Message[1]

ALLY DECIDED TO VENTURE BACK to the entrance of her garden, back to the place where she first saw the condition of her heart, and to her surprise it looked exactly the same. She frowned as she scanned the sad scenery surrounding her. She looked to the ground, where she had previously uncovered the little green shoot. It was still there, trying to smile at her but feeling very intimidated by the weeds still surrounding it.

The Garden Within

"New weeds come daily," she heard Jesus say.

She looked around but couldn't see Him.

"Therefore, weeding is a daily job," He said. His voice was coming from above her.

She looked up, and there He was, sitting on her garden wall. In his mouth was the shaft of a wheat stalk. He was chewing on the end.

"You kind of look like a farmer," Ally said as she giggled.

"That's the look I was aiming for," He said and smiled. He jumped down from His high place in her. "It looks like these weeds are suffocating our little friend here."

He bent down and pulled a few weeds to make room for this tiny plant to breathe. "Beware, Ally, of quick-growing weeds that try to spring up because of circumstances in your life. They will accumulate and try to destroy your garden."

He motioned for her to help Him.

"If you don't deal with these circumstances or problems in your life, they have a way of growing like these weeds here. And if you give them complete access to grow in your mind, these problems could become your lifestyle, and that lifestyle will suffocate all the good things that we have planted. If that life reigns, My life in you won't."

He bit His bottom lip, looked around her soul, and continued. "It's not enough to just love this garden life, Ally; you have to hate the weeds that try to choke the life from it."

Ally thought about that statement. *I hate the weeds I see choking the life from those around me—or choking me, myself. We have to hate the destroyer of life, peace, and joy. We need to despise those things that steal or choke our garden life, those things in life that sneak in and steal our time or joy.*

Jesus then said, "Weeds suffocate life; that is their job, and they are good at it. I have to teach you to recognize them. Then root out, pull up, and kill those weeds every day so that you can truly live. Freely live. As I said, weeding is a daily job, and sometimes a minute-by-minute job. You see, things like being offended plant a weed seed inside of you, and if you don't deal with it, it will grow and become difficult to pull up later." He came to a hearty weed that was planted in her heart. "Try to pull this one up," He said, pointing to it. Even at his pointing finger, this weed began to quiver.

Ally walked over to this haughty weed and grasped the base of it; although she pulled with all her might, this weed didn't budge.

"If you would have pulled this up when it was first planted in you, it would have been much easier, because the roots wouldn't have been deep yet."

Ally took a deep breath.

"If you remain in Me and walk with Me, I will point out the beginning of weeds. I see them. And if we pull them up when they are small, that is much easier than trying to pull larger weeds like this one."

Ally tried again by herself to pull up that stubborn weed. "I remember," she started, "when I had my first garden at home. I didn't always stay up on the weeding process. When I did, they were few and easy to pull, because they were small. But it seemed that even a few days would go by, and if I didn't tend my garden, I'd go out and *bam*—a ton of weeds!"

She again tugged with all her might at this huge weed in her soul and said, "I remember one that got so big, like this one, that I couldn't pull it by myself. The roots were too strong, and I needed someone stronger than me to pull it up."

Jesus replied, "Sometimes you need to find someone to pray with you in agreement to remove these obstinate weeds— maybe one who has walked with Me through something similar

The Garden Within

and because of that has become a little stronger than you. You see, I made my people to need one another and to help one another—just like I will use you to help pull up some things in other people's gardens."

Ally pushed her hair from her face. She had begun to sweat, trying to pull up this booger of a weed. "This big weed in my garden at home," she continued, though she was out of breath as she wiped some sweat from her brow. "There was no one around that I could find to help, so I took a hose."

She then grabbed a hose that was lying nearby that was being fed water from the River of Life in her. "And I ran water on this massive weed until the soil beneath it became mud. It took awhile for the water to get deep enough, but that made pulling it out by the root easier."

She continued watering at the base of this weed in her soul. "And I got this revelation from you, Lord, I believe," she said, smiling up at Him. "That the water of your Word, Your truth, softens the ground of my heart and loosens every wrongful thing planted there."

With that said, and with the water still running, she again yanked on this awful plant, and it came out of her, roots and all. As it did she fell on her backside because she was yanking so hard.

Jesus began laughing. "I love when you get it," He said, reaching out His hand to help her up. "My truth will set you free!"

Ally felt a sense of freedom in her that she had not felt in a long time. He lifted her up.

"It's gone," she said and smiled. "The bad feelings inside and the sorrow are all gone." She looked to the weed she had pulled out with truth. "Look at the size of that root!" she exclaimed. "No wonder it had remained in me for so long." She began to laugh and just couldn't stop until tears were running down her cheeks. "Thank You, Jesus."

The weed before her already had begun to wilt. That thing that had been so stately on the inside of her for so long and refused to surrender now just lay as a sad clump before her eyes. It was no longer imposing and no longer powerful.

"If you keep your mind and your thoughts on Me, I will kill the things that have tried to rule your life, the things that suffocate My life in you—like this weed here," He proclaimed, picking up the weed that Ally had just pulled from her heart. "This former tyrant master is dead. It shall not live or reappear, because you got the root lie out. It is now a powerless ghost. It shall not rise or come back again."

He then looked directly at the weed and said, "I will cause every memory and every trace of your so-called supremacy over this life to perish!" He threw the weed over the wall, and it was now totally out of her garden. "There is a war with weeds until I come and conquer them and until I replace them with Myself, and with My truth, through your surrender."

Truth had filled the hole left by that ugly weed.

GET TO THE ROOT

With this stronghold out of her life, Ally began pulling up the smaller weeds in her heart with ease. She had a new hope and new strength. Both she and Jesus were sitting in the midst of these surrounding weeds, and most of them took on the form of dandelions.

"You know how that weed finally came out, root and all?" Jesus asked. "If we pull the weeds but the roots remain, it will just allow that same weed to pop back up again."

As Jesus spoke, Ally pulled on a dandelion and heard that popping sound. "Oh, that is not good," she said. "That sound means that even though it *looks* like the weed is gone, the root remains embedded in the ground."

The next one she pulled came out roots and all. "Victory!" she shouted.

Jesus smiled in response to her victory shout.

Ally remembered mowing her lawn at her home, which had quite a few dandelions growing in it. Normally she just mowed them down because that was easier than pulling them out, and for a while, it looked like all was well. But they did come back, and they came back worse than before.

"Why, sometimes, do we try what we think is the easy way, Jesus?"

He had just taken the top off a weed and left the root, pointing to it. "Because they do seem gone, for a while, and it is easier to just snap the top off. But easy isn't always the best answer."

He dug a little deeper and pulled out the root He had just left. "Disciplining your thoughts, for instance, is hard work. Some people try to control their mouths, but they do nothing about their thoughts. That is like pulling off the top of a weed. Unless the root is dug up, the weeds always come back." He threw the root off to the side.

"Also, excuses, such as those for behaving badly, are like weeds. If left unattended they will choke the fruit, or life, in you. Self pity, envy, an unforgiving heart, bitterness, anger—all those will grow like bad weeds and choke what I am doing and want to do in your life." He looked around at the existing weeds.

Ally sighed and said, "This is hard work."

"But look how much we've done in just a short time already," He replied. He glanced around her heart and added, "But yes, it is hard work. But it will yield a harvest of righteousness and blessing as you continue. Continue with Me, and we will kindly pull up all these weeds!"

He pointed His finger toward the remaining weeds in her garden. "Make Me your habit, Ally. Daily you need to choose Me, to choose life, over and over and over again, until that becomes your habit. Imagine that!" He grinned. "A habit of joy, truth, abundant life, and peace."

Ally thought about the meaning of the word *habit*.

Jesus, knowing this, answered, "A habit is a constant, sometimes unconscious inclination to perform an act, and it is formed or acquired through its frequent repetition. You do it and do it and do it again."

"I want You to be my habit, Jesus," Ally replied.

"Then remain in Me, walk with Me daily, and let Me be your constant companion. You see, you are either walking with Me, in My presence, or you are walking in the flesh, which is your own way of thinking and doing. Like I said before, you don't have to work at being in the flesh. You don't work to plant weeds."

She looked to her feet, where weeds were still surrounding her. "Nope, I surely didn't plant these."

"Here is how I become your habit, Ally. Are you ready for this?"

He had her complete focus.

"Relate all of your life to God, to Me, our Father, and the Holy Spirit. Everything. Connect everything to God. Talk to Us. Interact with Us. Work with Us so that we can carry Our purpose for you in the world to its completion."

Ally was trying to really grasp what He was saying.

"Live in Our companionship, Ally. Companionship comes from the word *company*."

The Garden Within

Ally thought about the times when she invited company over. She smiled when she thought, *I am having God over tonight.*

"Live in the company of God; live in Our presence continuously. Spend time with Us, Ally."

A little finch landed on the wall above their heads and sang out a little song. "Again, relate all of your life to Us. Everything in your life, Ally—see it through Our eyes and through Our perspective. You see, you have a different perspective from down here, which basically means you have a different view. We know what we are doing, Ally. Ask for Our perspective."

Ally thought about how earlier that week she was in a crowd of people when she noticed a little girl pulling on her daddy's pant leg. "Lift me up, Daddy," the little girl had exclaimed. "I can't see from down here."

Wow, she thought, and then she looked at Jesus and said, "Pick me up, Jesus. I also cannot see from down here."

Jesus knew she was grasping His truth.

"Get Our thoughts on every situation." He continued, "Get Our perspective, Our guidance. Ask Me what I say or think about every situation."

He glanced around her heart. "Keep alert, Al. Watch for weeds, and be sensitive about what is going on in and around you. Be attentive to your garden life but also to the gardens surrounding you." He was speaking of other people in her life.

"Always ask yourself this question, as it will help you in life: 'Does this affect my intimacy with God?' That will help you to choose life and to live on purpose. You know, when you fully comprehend that there is more to life than just the here and now, and you realize that this life is just a training ground for eternity spent with Me, you will begin to live differently. That is Our perspective, Ally."

He spread His hands out wide. "You will begin to live in the reality of eternity, right here and now; and that will affect how you handle everything. Every relationship, task, situation, and circumstance. To make the most out of your life, keep the picture of eternity continuously in your mind, in your heart, and in your garden."

As He spoke those last words, Ally's heart became brighter with color. She watched as lilies bloomed before her eyes in yellow, pink and orange, and tulips lifted their faces in every color imaginable. Life was taking place in her. Truth was taking place in her. Love was in her and surrounding her. The fragrance from these blooms filled her garden and her senses—the very fragrance of Jesus Himself!

Jesus broke into her thoughts, saying, "Even surrounded by these blooms, Ally, beware, because you do have an Enemy. He will always try to plant weed seeds, even when things seem to be going so beautifully, and even while you are sleeping."

Ally remembered waking in the morning and looking at her garden at home only to find new weeds.

"The Enemy is after your testimony. He is after your flourishing garden life, and he is after these blossoms," He said as He raised His hands over the newly opened flowers. "He tried to ruin and destroy it with quick-growing weeds. He is trying to confuse and frustrate you, and he is committed to that. His goal is to try to thwart My purpose for your life. He himself is a weed."

He held His arms out to the sides, and immediately Ally saw the cross behind Him. His voice then resounded as He proclaimed, "We overcome the Enemy by the blood of the Lamb, Myself, and by the Word of our testimony. You overcome

The Garden Within

him, the Devil, by God's own power. God's power is released through you when you pray. Just talk to Him in everything. We are living on the inside of you, here in you."

She looked around and saw the beauty of the Lord everywhere.

"Your words, Ally, can be like weeds or like blooms. Your words can either suffocate the Enemy of your soul or oxygenate the Enemy of your soul—just by what you say." He reached out and touched her mouth. "By the words you speak, you bring life or death."

Oh Lord, may I always feel Your hand touching my lips and guarding my words, Ally thought.

"It's all a choice; even intimate friendship with Me is a choice, not an accident. You must spend time with the gardener, for I bring the change. When you seek Me, you will find Me, and we will tend to this garden. We will pull up the weeds together, and you will truly live."

They began walking and came to a part of her soul that looked pretty good. He sat down, and she sat next to Him.

"Say your garden is looking really good, and then something happens in your life. Maybe someone didn't validate you or said something as you perceived as mean to you, and these seeds of weeds began to take root, and they started squeezing the life out of all God has done."

Ally began to think of a situation in her life when someone had recently hurt her feelings.

"Here lies the problem," He explained, looking into her eyes. "Sometimes you tend to the problem more than you tend to the plantings of the Lord."

Ally nodded in agreement.

"To *tend* is to apply one's attention. Problems and circumstances try to steal your attention away from Me, away from love, and away from what I am doing in your garden."

Ally blew her breath up at her bangs, as she knew she had done that very thing—and quite often.

"You tend to talk more about the problems than the answers or truth. Others may try to plant weeds in you, and the world will try to steal your full attention. Don't let those weeds, those lies, or worldly things grow in your garden, because weeds spread quickly. Be watchful. Be attentive, because they will try to crowd out, take over, and steal the nutrients from the things I have planted in you."

He paused, looking very attentive to something He was hearing.

"My advice to your new weed-watching department," He said, pointing to her brain, "is to give new invaders high priority and stop them before they get out of hand." He was smiling, because He knew He was enough.

Inside of her, she knew also that this King was enough, and the new truths blossoming around and within her kept her heart focused on the one who planted them there.

Jesus then reached down and pulled a stone from the sole of His shoe. It was a gray, unattractive stone. "To add to the others," He said. "I chose an ugly stone to remind you that the weeds are unattractive. They won't attract others to Me if your life and your actions are surrounded by them."

Ally slowly took the stone from His hand, wrinkled her nose at it, and added it to her previously acquired stones. "I hope this is the only ugly one," she said and glanced up from her little black pouch.

"Remember this when you look at the weed stone: Love the flowers; hate the weeds. Love good and hate evil."

Ally closed her eyes and nodded in acknowledgment, and when she opened them she found herself lying under a cedar tree.

Chapter 11

Under the Cedar Tree

May Christ, through your faith, [actually] dwell (settle down, abide, make His permanent home) in your hearts! May you be rooted deep in love and founded securely on love, so that you may have the power and be strong to apprehend and grasp with all the saints [God's devoted people, the experience of that love] what is the breadth and length and height and depth [of it]; That you may really come to know [practically, through experience for yourselves] the love of Christ, which far surpasses mere knowledge [without experience]; that you may be filled, through all your being, unto all the fullness of God and become a body wholly filled and flooded with God Himself.
Ephesians 3:17–19

A LLY LAY ON THE GROUND in some lavish, green grass, looking up through the cedar's hearty branches. She looked to her side, and Jesus was lying beside her.

"Did you know that cedar is the strongest or hardiest type of wood there is?"

Ally shook her head and replied, "No, I did not."

"It is because of the tenacity of its roots. I want you to be rooted and grounded in Me, and I will make you strong like this cedar here."

Ally watched as these massive tree branches moved so elegantly in the gentle breeze that started blowing around them.

"I am going to teach you now about your thoughts, Ally. You need to train them to be rooted and founded in Me and Me alone, and I will make you strong and immovable. You need to learn to take every single thought that comes into your mind into captivity. What I mean by that is this: You do not need to let every thought that comes into your mind have full freedom in you. You do have a bit of control over your thoughts, if you do not let them take you everywhere they want to. You need to grab hold of them when they come in and restrain them. Don't let them just run freely through your mind, but grasp them firmly, and bring every one of them to Me."

Ally thought about how many thoughts had taken up residence in her mind and were roaming about, free and unrestrained.

"You need to deprive these thoughts of freedom and liberty and ask yourself these questions: Is this truth? Is this thought from God? Or does it come from the Enemy of my soul? Does this thought bring life or death? If death, then withstand these thoughts initially, when they first enter. Bring them to Me. Be rooted in Me and these truths I am teaching you, and you will be established, strong, and immovable, just like this cedar tree."

Ally looked again at the majestic tree and then found herself back in the vineyard with Jesus. It had perfect rows of grapevines growing on the inside of her.

They came upon a wild vine branch that had grown away from the main vine. She knew that the main vine was a symbol of Jesus Himself because of the scripture that talked about Him being the true vine.

Jesus continued talking as He took this wild vine, brought it back, and attached it to the main vine. As He did this He said, "Don't think and set your feelings on the thoughts the Enemy puts in your mind and let them have free rein in you. But bring them back and attach them to the sturdy, stable, fixed, sure vine—the truth. Me. Attach every thought to Me. And we will cut off and remove all that is not truth, but lies. Set your mind and keep it set on what is above, the higher things, and not on the things that are of the earth."

"What do you mean by set my mind?" Ally asked, trying to apply this truth.

Jesus then fastened the wild vine firmly with some wire that He retrieved from His pocket. "*Set* means to put in a specific position or state or to put in a stable position. It means to fix, so fix your thoughts on Me, Ally." He smiled with His eyes. "It means to restore to a proper and normal state when dislocated or broken, like setting a bone when an arm is broken."

"Some of my thinking is broken, I'm sure."

"Yes, sometimes your mind or thoughts are a little dislocated. They are thrown into confusion or disorder when they are disrupted by lies. You know, Ally, the Enemy of your soul wants to disrupt the flow and the plan of God for you. He wants to throw you into confusion, put you out of proper relationship, and displace you. He wants to put you in a place of doubt."

Ally thought about how frequently doubt and insecurity took up residence in her thoughts.

"Bring every thought before Me, and I will adjust those thoughts for proper functioning. I will put you in a stable position that is resistant to sudden changes and to the negative thoughts that the Enemy plants. When negative thoughts first come, at the beginning of an attack on your mind, be firm and immoveable. Right then set your thoughts on Me, on My truth. Fasten those thoughts to Me."

He came upon another vine that was running wild in her vineyard. "You see, these thoughts seek to devour you and this garden life. They seek your time and your devotion. The Enemy wants to take up residence in your thought life. He wants his lies to live in you, and he is very subtle, so he sneaks in. Guard your garden, and guard your thoughts."

She took in a deep breath as Jesus continued.

"Ally, let Me tell you a story. I once went by the field of a lazy man and by the vineyard of a man devoid of understanding. I was in another garden, and behold, it was all grown over with thorns. Nettles were covering its face, and its stone wall was broken down. Then this man beheld Me and considered what he was letting control his life. He received instruction, and his garden came back to life. Don't be lazy about taking your thoughts captive, or they could take over your garden."

Again, Ally considered how she had let her garden get so weed-filled and overcrowded with wrong thoughts.

"Spend time with Me, Ally; get understanding, and you will truly live. It takes a little work to take every thought into captivity, but be strong and encourage yourself in Me. Ask for My thoughts and My perspective, and I will give them to you."

The Garden Within

They walked up to a dry, withered shrub.

"If the lazy man had not turned his mind, thoughts, and heart to Me, he would have remained like a shrub destitute in the desert. He would not have seen any good come, but he would have dwelled in the parched, dry places in the wilderness and in uninhabited, salty land."

The shrub then totally transformed before their eyes into a strong tree with lots of fruit hanging from its branches.

"But instead, he believed in Me and trusted in Me. He made Me his hope and his confidence. And now, because he has stopped letting his thoughts run free in him and relies on Me, he shall be like a tree planted by the waters that spreads out its roots by the river. He, like you now, Ally, will not see and fear when heat comes; his and your leaves shall be green. You will not be anxious and full of care, and you will not cease yielding fruit. The people of this world need Me, Ally; they are dying. I want to feed them as I am feeding you. Will you hold out to the world this truth, this life? Will you live your life to give Me out to them? I am the fruit in you. I am the way and the truth, and I am this life."

As He said this, He pulled off a piece of fruit from the tree before them.

"They need Me. They may not know it yet, but they will. I put in all humankind this void that only I can fill. Can I use you? To hold out life?"

He handed Ally the fruit; they began walking, and He continued to talk about thoughts.

"If you sow good thoughts in the soil of your mind, the fruit that comes from it will be life giving and nourishing to yourself and to others."

She looked at the fruit in the palm of her hand. *Life,* she thought.

"Think about *what* you are thinking, Ally, because your life will move in the direction of your strongest thoughts. If you don't manage this thought life"—He paused to catch her gaze—"you won't manage your life. Don't continue to allow negative thoughts to manage your life anymore. Choose, Ally, to close your thoughts to the things you cannot change, and move forward. There are too many good things in life to allow things beyond your control to destroy you and your garden life. Don't choose to follow bad thoughts any further, because they will lead you down a path of destruction."

Jesus turned, and they began to move in a different direction. "Rather, decide to change direction again and again and again. Choose life and good thoughts until that becomes your habit."

Ally continued to follow Him; in every footstep she was witnessing His life continuing to form in her.

"Do you know what repentance is? It is when you decide to choose life and you turn your life and move in a different direction. It is to think differently than you used to think. Change your life, turn to Me, and walk this new direction with Me, like you just did, and new fruit will come."

Ally again looked at the piece of fruit in her hand.

"You can feed this fruit to others and help them live again."

They found themselves again under the cedar tree. Ally thought about Jesus first telling her that the cedar was the strongest tree because of its strong root system.

Jesus then asked, "Ally, do you see the roots?"

Ally shook her head. "No," she replied.

"That is because they are underground, unseen by others. Roots are the part of the tree or plant that serves as its support. Roots draw food for the plant and water from surrounding soil, and they also store food. It's the secret place, unseen by others, where it is just you and Me. Just like these roots, the secret place and that time with just the two of us is the base, support, or root source of the life I am creating in you. It is an essential part of this garden life and is needed for growth."

Ally adored this new garden life and this new relationship with her beloved. She loved the life she now felt inside her. She actually felt beautiful. She said, "I want the roots of my being and who I am to be firmly and deeply planted in You. Never before have I felt this beautiful or this alive, and it's You, Lord. It's all You."

Tears began to fall onto her cheeks as she looked into His big, brown eyes. "Keep me so rooted in You that the Enemy cannot get to those deep inner thoughts of my heart anymore. I want to remain wrapped up in You, for I belong to You."

Jesus smiled, because her last statement tied into the next meaning of what it meant to be rooted in Him that He wanted to share with her.

"Being rooted is being settled into, or belonging to. You do belong to Me. I bought you with My precious blood, and you and so many others belong to the family of God. Many times you asked, 'Where do I belong, God?' Well, you belong with Me, with Us."

Ally smiled and thought about the significance of the word *belong*.

"It also means to be fully settled or entrenched. The secret place in Me, Ally, is like a trench, and a trench is especially used for the purpose of fortifying and defending. It is a place of security. You are secure in Me. In this place I will strengthen you. I will add more and more strength, and I will provide moral and mental strength by adding extra support—just like the roots of this tree."

He placed His hand on her heart. "Here in the secret place I will give life to you, and I will fill you with strength and courage. I will inspire you here, and I will guide you by divine influence. I will fill you with noble and reverent emotion, and I will stimulate you to creativity and action. I will breathe life into you here so that you can then impart this life." He held up Ally's hand, which still had the piece of fruit in it, and said, "Feed my sheep, Ally. Bring them into My presence and into this way of life. I don't want any to perish, but I want all to come to this place of life and security."

Ally closed her eyes and held the piece of fruit with both hands, and again she saw a sea of faces before her. She began to encourage them with these words.

"When circumstances and situations surround you that seem dark and dreary, jump into God's trench. It's like an army's trench but safer. You are so safe there. Jump into the garden, the secret place, His trench, and let Him fortify you there. When the Enemy is shooting his fiery darts at you, jump into the trench! Jump into the secret place and let God invigorate you. Let Him impart His strength and courage to you! Let Him breathe His life into you and give you life. Let Him fill you with His Spirit and inspire you to be active on His behalf! Let Him guide and arouse you by His divine influence! Let Him fill you with reverent emotion and stimulate you to creativity and action! Let Him defend you, for He is your Defender. Let Him protect you and keep you. Let Him live in you and for you!"

She could actually feel His life flowing from her being, just like He said when He told her about His rivers flowing from her. "Being rooted in Him like this is necessary for growth. Stay attached to the sure vine and to the truth. You cannot truly live without being rooted deeply in Him and in His love."

The Garden Within

She ended her encouraging words with this firm statement: "You are loved."

Ally was amazed by the crowd of hearts that stood before her. She could actually see them being transformed before her. She saw some weeping, some laughing, and some praying, but all of them were grasping the truth she was revealing to them.

When this vision ended, she opened her eyes and saw that the fruit in her hand had turned into her eighth stone. Yellow in color, and it looked like it had roots running through it. She slipped her little black pouch out of her pocket and added to it this new precious stone.

Rooted in Him, she thought. She looked around her heart, her garden. She couldn't see Jesus any longer, but she knew that He was still with her, and the fruit tree remained.

Strong.

Immovable.

Chapter 12

You Look Just Like Your Dad

Behold, as the clay is in the potter's hand, so are you in My hand.
Jeremiah 18:6

THE NEXT AFTERNOON, IN THE soft breezes of a lovely summer day, Ally tended the garden at her house. She came upon a dahlia that had been crushed and lay lifeless at her feet. She was perplexed by the devastation of this once tall, upright, beautiful flower.

At once she found herself before a door which had an antique, rounded top that appeared to have been made from different pieces of rosewood crafted together. In the middle of the door, on a golden plate, was the inscription "Potter's House" and below that an invitation to "Come In."

As she pushed open the heavy door, she saw Him, the one whom her soul loved. He was working at the potter's wheel,

The Garden Within

spinning a beautiful pot. She watched Him as He so lovingly and delicately shaped this vessel with His hands. He pulled up on the sides so as to make it taller and smoother. He dipped His hands in a bucket to get more water and returned to His masterpiece.

Suddenly, the piece He was making began to wobble and fall apart in His hands, so He made it over, reworking it into another vessel as it seemed good for Him to make. He then lifted His beautiful, shining eyes to meet Ally's focused, unbroken gaze.

"Can I do with you, Ally, as I have done with this vessel? Can I remake you? For as this clay is in My hands, so are you in My hands."

"Um", she paused for a second, "but you just crushed that vessel into a lump of clay. Will it hurt, Lord?"

"It will only hurt your ways of doing and being. For I know what I have planned for you, Ally. Can you trust Me? Will you just crawl into My hands and let Me mold you into the vessel that will escort you into your destiny?"

Ally's face fell, as she was a little apprehensive to answer His question.

"I have known what I have been making you, Ally, through all you have been through already. Sometimes you have wanted to look like others or be like others and have strived with Me. You have said to the One fashioning you, 'What do You think You are making?' or 'Where are my handles?'"

Ally immediately thought of a time when she desired to be like someone else and had compared herself to this person.

"I never intended my vessels to compete with each other; I want you to complete each other—to celebrate and encourage each other's strengths while finding out who I created you to be."

Ally looked up at some shelving that was filled with a lot of different vessels. Some were tall and slender, some were shorter and wider, and some were painted and shiny. Still other vessels had just recently been shaped by the Master's hand and were waiting to go into the fire so that they would retain their shape forever.

Jesus walked over to a big basin and began washing His hands. He looked back at Ally with a sneaky grin on His face and then turned and splattered her with the water left on His hands. It took her by surprise that He could be so serious yet so much fun all at the same time. She giggled as she wiped her face with her hand, keeping her gaze locked on Him.

He then nodded His head at her, indicating she should follow Him into the next room.

They entered, and her breath was taken away. Before them was the most brilliant table she had ever seen. It had every kind of flower, tree, and plant she had ever laid eyes on, plus ones she'd never seen carved into the surface of the table. Not a flaw was on this table, for it was perfectly formed by a master craftsman.

"This is my Father's table," Jesus said, "and I made it for Him. It is a place of revelation, and it is a place of introducing realities—a place where you receive your true identity."

He pulled out a chair. "Sit," He invited.

Ally's eyes grew huge as she looked at Him, and she slowly sat in the chair He had pulled out for her. Then He gently pushed her up to the table.

In her heart, she heard, *"Find your identity in Him."*

On the table before her was a small golden vial with the word *spikenard* written across it in silver pewter.

With tears welling up in His eyes, Jesus said, "This spikenard is a costly fragrance, and the plant must be crushed in order to

The Garden Within

make this perfume. Only then is the oil extracted. It represents worship. God, the Father, loves Me and wants to give Me a beautiful bride who loves Me extravagantly. You are at His table right now, sitting with Me, your groom to be."

Ally closed her eyes and saw the picture of the cross with Jesus crushed, bruised, and bleeding before her. She grabbed the small vial before her and drank the perfume. She really didn't understand why, but she knew that she wanted worship to be in her. She wanted this costly perfume that He'd paid for with the stripes He took for her at the cross to come alive inside of her vessel.

"Your identity is who you are to Me. Ally, come to this table often and revelation will come. Revelation is the clear and often sudden ability to really understand the things I have to say to you, or that I want you to learn. These things are covered right now but will be revealed as you come. This table of revelation is for unearthing something that has been covered. It will be a place of greater insight and discovery for you. I will make Myself known here. I will fill you with light here and cause you to shine; then you can in turn give out that light. It is a place of spiritual understanding or insight of Me."

Ally looked into the polished surface of the table and saw her reflection shining back at her.

"Here is the first revelation."

Once again His words captured her attention.

"You are made in Our image. At My table this truth will become a reality to you so that when you go out in your community, they will say of you, 'You look just like your Father.' That is what happens here; you begin to take on Our characteristics and Our behaviors because you have been here. You know you become like those you spend time with. You will look like Me to the world when you spend time with Me.

I will fashion you as I have these pots," He said, looking up at the finished vessels that also filled the shelves in this room, "to look just like Me."

Ally felt excitement flow through her whole body.

"May I tell you a little about what it means to be made in Our image, the image of the Father, the Son, and the Holy Spirit?"

Ally loved being at this table of revelation, for it felt as if life itself, His life, was filling her. "Yes," she replied.

"An image is the reproduction of the form of someone," He said and then grabbed a vessel of gold from a shelf. "For example, a sculptured likeness." He took His sleeve and rubbed a little smudge off the surface of it. "When I say reproduction, that is something that is reproduced, or made again, from the original."

He put His hand on His chest, lifted His head high, and said, "I am the original." He looked back down at her and grinned. "It also means something duplicated, which means it's identically copied from an original or from a close or exact resemblance of another. So *resemblance* means similar in nature, form, and appearance, and to have a likeness to. It is as if someone were to say, 'You act just like your dad.'"

He set the vessel on the table. "Another meaning of *reproduce* is *imitate*, like an imitative appearance. You know, like Elvis?"

That caught Ally off guard. Of course—why wouldn't He know about Elvis and his impersonators? She laughed as Jesus stood up and did His best Elvis impersonation with His legs, dancing around her.

"They come in, and they look like him, act like him, move like him, and sing like him." He stopped dancing. "I want you to imitate Me." He sat back down with her at the table. "Here is the meaning of *imitate*."

The Garden Within

Ally was smiling, she greatly loved this table of Him, revealing truth to her.

"*Imitate* means to model oneself after the behavior or actions of another or to copy or mimic someone's actions, appearance, mannerisms, or speech. It means to copy exactly, to resemble, or to picture mentally and imagine. Picture yourself like Me, for you are, Ally, made in My image. When you spend time with Me in the garden and at this table, you will begin to look like Me, act like Me, and talk like Me." He smiled at her.

She smiled back as she began to imitate Him. He rested His chin upon His hand, and she did the same. He then made prayer hands and lifted them to His nose, and she did the same. He scratched His head and Ally mimicked that. Jesus then threw back His head and gave a big belly laugh.

"You are so silly," He said, and they laughed together.

"You see, Ally, My desire is to reproduce Myself to the world. And I do so through you and the rest of My children. I want to set Myself on display through you, to give evidence of or demonstrate My love, My grace, My goodness, and My power to the world through you and other vessels that I have made."

He stood, pulled her closer, turned her around to face outward with His hands on her shoulders, and said, "I want to present you to the world and say, 'Look, here is My daughter, made in My image. She will give evidence of Me, and by My presence within her, she will demonstrate My love, My character, and My likeness to the world.'"

Ally looked over her shoulder at Jesus and smiled.

"It's a time of presentation, Ally—to present My chosen ones to the world, to those around them. And this is a very specific time for a presentation of Me, saying of you, 'This is My daughter.' Now walk in it."

Ally was amazed at Him in her. She literally felt as if He were in her—His very life living her life.

"That's because it *is* Me, Ally."

She put her hand over her heart and took a deep breath. *Oh yeah, He knows all my thoughts.*

"At this table, and in your garden, We are making you into a vessel of honor. When you are here, you are cultivating a friendship with Me and with the Father. Come to this table of revelation often, and We will pour into your vessel everything that is needed for your journey. Let Me see your stones," He said, holding out His hand.

Ally reached into her pocket and pulled out her little pouch of stones. She handed it to Jesus.

He poured them out on the table and picked up the little black stone, the first one He had presented her with. "Do you remember your dark but comely stone?" He held it out for her to take. "Do you know what makes you comely to Me? Lovely to Me? It is not in your performance, Ally; your loveliness is found in the image of Me and in a willing heart that longs for Me. You were created to be like Me. You were destined from the beginning to be molded into the image of the Son and share inwardly My likeness."

Ally grabbed a little pink vessel from a shelf and put her small fist inside of it. She felt the smoothness of its interior as she spoke, saying, "I want to be like You on the inside."

Jesus smiled wide and said, "In the garden of your soul, as you spend time with the gardener, Me, I will fashion your insides to be like Me, as well as the outside. I will change your countenance and your behaviors. We will fashion your life to resemble Ours."

Ally stood up and began twirling and dancing, and said, "So others will say of me, 'She looks just like her Dad.'"

Jesus was thrilled to see her taking on the shape and form He planned for her.

"Your loveliness and beauty came from the gift of righteousness that became yours when you first believed in Me."

She continued to twirl; she had so much joy, just like a little girl who found out she was really a princess. "I am lovely because of what You did for me, not what I do for You. For I have a loving King"—she curtsied before Him—"who gave away His beauty to take away my ugliness and insecurities. It is through Your sacrifice that I am made lovely and beautiful in Your sight."

He enjoyed watching the dance of her life. "Ally, that day when you turned to Me, and said yes to Me, the work of the Holy Spirit made you lovely in My sight. I want you to know that I will always see you not in your weakness, but will see My grace on the inside of your heart. I see the beauty of My life forming within you."

He pulled her to Him, knelt before her, and placed His hands on her stomach. "You see, you possess on the inside of you, in the most secret and hidden places of your heart, your garden, your life, beautiful virtues that will one day be seen by all. You won't be able to contain them, because you will be so full of Me. Right now they may be just seeds, those things I have planted in you, those dreams, those visions. If you continue to water and tend to your garden, if you continue to let the gardener work in you, in time those seeds will spring up into magnificent beauty for your Bridegroom. This image, My image, is growing in you, being fashioned in you, and reflecting back to Me and to those who surround you. I see the beauty of My life being formed in your eyes."

"Today, Lord," Ally said, "I am transformed by Your extravagant love!" She put both of her hands over her heart and said, "The day will come when my garden will be so refreshing and my life will not be lived to impress others, but will become the overflow of Your life living in me. For You are truly living on the inside of me, and You are making me into a vessel of honor, to pour Your life into others."

With that, she spun with her face lifted high and found herself back in her small plot of land in her earthly garden. And there on the ground before her, where the crushed dahlia had been, was that little, pink vessel she had held back at her Father's table. On the inside was a small, folded note.

When she unfolded it, a small, beautiful purple stone fell out. She heard His voice in her heart say, "Royalty. Purple stands for royalty." Again she felt like a princess. She looked at the note, which had clearly come from Jesus; it read, "You look just like your Dad."

Chapter 13

I Will Change Your Name

He knows my name, what He calls me, when we commune with Him, He reveals who we really are.

He who is able to hear, let him listen to and heed what the Spirit says. To him who overcomes, I will give to eat of the manna that is hidden, I will give him a white stone with a new name engraved on the stone, which no one knows or understands except he who receives it.
Revelation 2:17

THE FOLLOWING MORNING, ALLY AWOKE early, hearing the voice she was coming to know so well speak to her heart. "And you shall be called by a new name, which the mouth of the Lord shall name, and this new name that I have for you is who you really are."

Ally grew excited to get up and spend some time at the table she'd visited the day before to understand what these words meant. She showered, made herself a dry cappuccino drizzled with caramel, her favorite, and sat down in her big leather chair. She grabbed her Bible and asked with great anticipation, "What do you call me, Lord?"

Suddenly she found herself not in her garden, but in a garden far more beautiful and far more colorful than she had ever even imagined. It was teeming with life—actually, it was *breathing* life. It was occupied with brilliant flowers that surrounded her and that she knew did not grow on the earth. The colors of this place were beyond her own vocabulary. *Vibrant* was the only word she could think of.

Could it be, she thought, *that this is a garden in heaven?*

"Exactly."

She turned to see Jesus. He looked a bit different than when she had seen Him in her own garden. He looked kingly and simply dignified, and the light that shone around Him was almost blinding.

"Did I die?" Ally asked apprehensively.

Jesus laughed. "No, We just wanted to bring you here today, to Eden, because We want to give you something from here."

Ally was astonished at her surroundings; they almost seemed to be like an animated movie. All the flowers appeared to be alive—alive like a human, with personality and character. She realized that she couldn't even put her thoughts into words to describe the beauty that she found herself in.

"We want to give you a new name."

Oh my goodness, Ally thought as she remembered the Word she had woken up to.

"The new name that You have for me will reveal who I really am, right?"

Jesus was thrilled because He knew that her spirit had heard His voice that morning as she lay in bed.

"Yes, I want to tell you what We call you. Many of Our children will not receive or know their new name until they get here, to heaven. But there are a few to whom We reveal their new names earlier so as to mold them into the character of that name while they are still on the earth. It is to shape them, so to speak, for their work on the earth."

Ally's mind went to the ones whose names God changed in the Scriptures, so what He was telling her was beginning to make sense. Her excitement grew to hear this new name.

"Peter, Jacob, Sarah, and Abraham are ones you have heard of, right?" Jesus asked. Then, seeing her nod, He continued, "But did you know about these? Joshua, Paul, Barnabas, Barsabbas, Thaddaeus, or Mark? And then there were James and John, I liked to call those two *Boanerges*, which means "Sons of Thunder." I renamed them all! You see, I enjoy naming my children; it makes them who they really are, who I created them to be. It reveals to them their true identity."

Ally was still astonished by her surroundings, but more so by Jesus and the brightness of His countenance.

"In obedience, as you begin to use your new name, you will see a change immediately. For your character will change, and your demeanor will change." He noticed Ally's expression as she tried to remember what that word *demeanor* meant.

"The way you act," He explained, smiling.

"Got it." Ally nodded.

He continued, saying, "Even your countenance will change—the way you look, both to yourself and to others."

Ally smiled at Him.

"You see, this new name will bring you out of the captivity you have been in, and it will give you a new view of yourself. For example, I doubt that Sarai, whom you know as Sarah in the Bible, saw herself as a princess, which is what *Sarah* means. She needed to see herself differently. By giving her a new name, I began the process of helping her to see herself in a new way. She began to take on the characteristics of that new name and therefore was made into another image, the image of whom I said she was. It was the same for her husband, Abram, whom I named Abraham, the father of many nations. Each time their names were spoken by other people, their futures were being prophesied or changing to fulfill their destiny. I remade them and refashioned them, just like you saw Me do to that vessel on the wheel yesterday. Changing their names began that process.

I am also shaping you, Ally. I have a new place for you, and every time someone calls you by your new name, they will be prophesying who you really are, and that will shape your future."

Ally's anticipation continued to grow, and she smiled at Jesus.

"I can transform lives in many ways, but one way that I love is to do it by changing names."

"Won't people think I am weird?"

"They already do." Jesus nudged her, and they laughed together.

"But in all seriousness, here's the thing, Ally—if you are obedient and you do this, if you go by this new name, the process will deliver you from the opinions of man."

Ally thought about that statement; she had lived most of her life worrying about what people thought about her. *Oh, to be free from that would be amazing.*

The Garden Within

It was then she asked, "What do You call me?"

Jesus smiled and walked over to her. He then pulled up a lily that was dancing on the hillside, handed it to her, and said, "Zoe. We call you Zoe."

The instant she heard the name, peace flooded her soul, and it brought an immediate confidence in the fact that He had changed her name.

"This is a descriptive name," He continued. "I want to transmit to you a mental image of who you really are, who We made you to be."

"Zoe," she said, pondering the name.

"You are going to be one who helps others become whole. You will help them to live again, to truly live the abundant life that I came to give them. Do you realize that this is what I have been teaching you in the garden of your soul and in this garden of Eden?"

She thought back on all that He had taught her.

"You have heard and watched Me teach things to you, and you have changed. Now I entrust you to pass them down onto others so that they will grow into all I have for them and will themselves teach others. You see, I have been molding you for a life-giving purpose. I will cause you to flourish, and this is what I see: I see you walking by others' gardens, which will begin to flourish instantly. I am giving you not only a brand-new name, but also a brand-new life. My life in you will change you and others."

She already felt a new vibrancy inside. The new name was life giving.

"Do you remember when we first entered your garden, Zoe?"

He called me Zoe, she thought, feeling more change.

"How it looked to be dead and like all life was gone?"

"Ah, yes, how could I forget?" she replied.

"There are many broken people in the world and even in your life now. Things or circumstances came into their lives, whether through their own choosing or not, and they left their lives devastated. Whether self-inflicted or otherwise, they feel forsaken, lost, and dead. They feel devastated, and they think that they are desolate and without hope—just like you felt."

Her heart saddened. She knew exactly what that felt like, for she had experienced that very thing.

"I want to come into their lives just as I came into yours. I want to replace their mourning with joy. I want to restore the years the Enemy has taken and rebuild the places he destroyed, leaving them feeling desolate and alone. I want to give them life."

Zoe thought again about the condition of her soul when they first entered her garden.

"As you give what you've been given, as you live and walk in Me, it will cause others to want to walk in Me and live in Me also."

She drew in her breath, and held it while she smiled.

"I gave you life, Zoe. Now give it away." As He said this, He handed her a white, polished stone, and across it, one word was written.

Zoe

Chapter 14

Fruit

With Me (God) is the fruit found which is to nourish you.
Hosea 14:8 "From Me comes your fruit." (ESV)

It is a joy to Jesus when a person takes time to walk more intimately with Him. The bearing of fruit is always shown in Scripture to be a visible result of an intimate relationship with Jesus Christ.
Oswald Chambers[1]

"GIVE LIFE AWAY." THOSE WORDS hung in Zoe's mind as she walked through the rest of her day, clutching the white stone with her new name written across it.

"In knowing Me, you become like Me."

She heard His voice as if He were standing right in the room with her. She had spent the day getting some things done around her house. She had also meditated on the time she'd spent that morning in the secret place—this time, in the Garden of Eden with her beloved Jesus. And once again, He was conversing with her.

"It's much more than knowing about Me."

Zoe was immediately in her garden again, this time surrounded by an orchard of apple trees. *His voice is coming from up inside one of these trees,* she thought, and she continued to follow the sound. She then looked up into one of the trees and saw His feet dangling down.

He lowered down a basket filled with apples from a little pulley that He had rigged to get the apples from high in the tree to the ground without bruising them.

Zoe grabbed the basket as it got closer to her and set it gently on the ground.

"Again, I can't say this enough—it is about spending time with Me here in the secret place, the garden of your soul." He began to climb down the tree to her. "It's getting to know My love for you, My mercy, and My character in very personal and real ways."

He took the final jump out of the tree and stood right before her. "This is eternal life—that you would know Me and also that you would know our Father who sent Me to the world. This is how I lived on the earth: in constant fellowship with Him. And I want you to have constant and continuing fellowship with Me. I know that is how you will produce lots of life-giving fruit." He reached down and picked up the full basket of apples on the ground. "Knowing Me and living this life in Me produces much fruit that will nourish lives wherever you go."

"So this fruit is a visible result of intimacy with You?" Zoe reached down and pulled an apple from the basket.

"Yes," He responded, "with the purpose of showing the Father fully on the earth. Live in the Spirit every day, always aware of what He is doing and saying in every situation, and then join Him in the work that He has for you on the earth. This takes intimate time spent in the secret place."

Zoe began to polish the apple on her pants.

"Intimacy with God, the Father, Myself, and the Holy Spirit always produces fruit, life, and nourishment—not only for you, but also for others."

She held the apple to her face and saw her reflection in its glossy surface. She then set her gaze back on Jesus.

"You see, Our desire is for everyone who believes to be fruitful. That was the plan from the very beginning: to be fruitful and to multiply. Our heart is that your lives and your gardens would germinate life in you and in all that you do."

"Germinate?" she questioned.

"To cause growth, to sprout, to begin to grow. To plant seeds in others. We want you to live a life that causes others to want that same life—a life of intimacy."

Zoe thought back on her conversation with her friends at the coffee shop. After she had shared her heart about her beloved, and after they had watched her countenance change before them, they too wanted what she had.

"That is the Spirit of multiplication: when others see and taste of the fruit you share, they will want their own fruit."

Zoe's mind went back to whom she had been and the change that spending time with Jesus brought. "I know for me"—she looked at Him—"I had to surrender who I was, my old unrenewed self. That true surrender and vulnerability to You brought intimacy with You. You loved me in my unrenewed state because You saw the potential of Your life in me."

Jesus smiled at her, and touched her cheek. "And that intimacy produced fruit in you, Zoe, and that fruit causes multiplication."

"Be fruitful and multiply," Zoe said. "Your fruit causes others to want what nourishes the soul, the mind, and the heart. Seeing your fruit in me causes people to want You. For Your fruit brings life—a life filled with love, joy, peace, patience, faithfulness, goodness, kindness, gentleness, and self-control."

As Zoe heard again the fruit that comes from the very heart and Spirit of God, she began to see in her own life the abundance of the fruit that she knew only came from spending intimate time with the lover of her soul.

"There is a very important aspect of this fruitful life, Zoe," Jesus said as He emptied the full basket into a nearby cart.

He captured her attention because she had recognized in His tone that the next words from His mouth were of great worth.

"You must remain in Me. Live your life in Me. As a branch cannot bear fruit all by itself, neither can you unless you remain in Me."

He walked back up to the tree, picked up the shears that he had used earlier in her garden, and cut off a branch that was heavy with fruit. "Cut off from Me, you produce nothing. You need to stay focused on the source of true life. In all of your uncertainties and insecurities, the only guarantee for having peace in your heart and fruit in your life is to remain in My love."

He grabbed her hand, and she felt pierced in her heart as He held it. Looking into her big, brown eyes, He said, "My love surpasses all other love. My love is compassionate: it heals, forgives, and reassures. It is a love that gives you life. Being cut off from this love leaves you disheartened and disconnected, and eventually everything in you will die. Stay in Me, Zoe." As He said these last words, tears formed in His eyes and started to flow down His cheeks. He was pleading with her to stay in Him.

Why would anyone ever want to leave this kind of love? she wondered. She reached out her hand and wiped His cheeks as her own tears now flowed from her eyes.

He so loved her heart, saying, "When you stay in Me, you become like Me; you will begin to take on My characteristics. In staying, you are conformed and transformed into My very image."

She again saw her reflection in His eyes.

"This intimacy that you are experiencing right now not only brings joy and fruitfulness, but also proves that you are being changed into My image, into My very likeness. You are becoming an extension of who I am—a shoot that, when joined with others, will fill the whole earth with My love."

Zoe again thought of her heart's condition when she had first met with Jesus, and she had an aha moment. She looked at Him and said, "You have caused me to be fruitful in the land of my affliction. In all my hurt and pain, I spent time with You in my garden. Instead of just running to the world for help, I ran to You." Tears began to flow again. "It was there You healed me, Lord, in the secret place."

He wiped her tears, replying, "You know, before you were ever born, I knew your journey, and I knew the fruit that would be birthed and find its home in you because of that journey. It was your journey to wholeness."

Zoe nodded.

"Some of the things you went through were tough, really hard things, but you now have fruit to share with others who have gone through some of those things, to help them and to nourish them back into wholeness."

Jesus grabbed a nearby hose, attached it to a deep-root-watering device, and pushed it into the ground at the base of one of her trees in the orchard. It would provide the tree's root system with water.

"I am your keeper, and I have been watering you every moment of your life. I have been watering with a strong purpose for your life: that my truths would take root and change your life and that your life would blossom, send forth shoots, and fill the whole world with the fruit of knowledge of the one true God."

"And with you, the fruit is found," she responded.

Jesus reached high into the tree and then told Zoe, "Hold out your hands."

She reached out her cupped hands to Him.

With that, He began to drop many colored stones from His hands into hers, and her hands were filled to overflowing. "Be fruitful, Zoe, and multiply as these stones are multiplying before you."

She began to laugh at the abundance in her hands, and suddenly she was again in her humble little home. She looked down into her palm, and one very colorful stone remained.

"I will abide and be fruitful," she said, smiling up towards the heavens. "I will hold out Your life, this fruit You have given to me to nourish others."

She pulled out her little black pouch and added the fruit stone to the others.

She knew that He was smiling back at her.

CHAPTER 15

Crossing the Jordan

Truly the Lord has given all the land into our hands.
Joshua 2:24

ZOE ROSE EARLY THE NEXT morning to the words, "Follow Me."

"Where are you?" she responded. Again she found herself before the River of Life in her garden. She looked across the river to notice Jesus standing on the other side.

"Follow Me," He again proclaimed.

"But how do I get over to You?" she asked as she looked to her left and to her right. She did not see any place where the river would allow her to cross, as it was moving rapidly and flowing over its banks.

Jesus shouted from the other side this proclamation: "This day I will begin to magnify Myself in you in the sight of all, so they may know that I am with you as I was with so many before."

He stepped a bit closer to the river. "You will know, Zoe, that the living God is with you wherever you go. You will also have a keen awareness of Me, because I will go before you and you will know it."

He stepped into the river and said, "Come over to this land."

At that, the river, which was just overflowing its banks, stood still far off upstream, and the ground before her became instantly dry. She stood still herself, astonished.

Again He spoke, saying, "Come into your promise."

And Zoe stepped by faith into the dry riverbed and advanced, not only to her Jesus, but also to her purpose in life. After she stepped out of the bed, her beloved lifted her up in the air, turned, and set her into His land. With that the waters of the river returned to their place and flowed over its banks as before.

"Remember when I first showed you this river, Zoe?"

"Yes," she said, nodding.

"Remember that in this life-giving river was the promise and that as you crossed through it you would receive everything you needed for life and godliness?"

"I do," she responded.

With confidence in His voice, He spoke. "Today it has been fulfilled. I have given you everything today that you need for the rest of your journey on this earth and in your world. It's in the crossing that you have received. Today you will know that My hand has shaped and restored your life completely."

Zoe looked down, and her attire had changed from her jeans and T-shirt to a beautiful, white wedding gown. She remembered the words He had spoken to her that first time at the river: "Forever, your life and My life in you will cause others to want Me and worship Me."

She looked down into the river, and she saw the beautiful gown and the glow on her face reflecting back at her. "I am whole," she proclaimed. "You have remade me with Your love." She paused. "You have transformed me to look like You."

She knew her physical form looked nothing like Him, yet her spirit was renewed inside of her.

Jesus held out His hand to her, and in it was her little black pouch of memorial stones that she had collected from Him on her journey.

"To you, these stones shall forever be a reminder that you are made with a purpose that only you and I together can fulfill."

She received the pouch from His hand but kept unbroken eye contact with Him.

"This is the Promised Land. This journey has been about restoration, breakthrough, and crossing over into all that We have promised you and planned for you to do for Us. All of Our promises are fulfilled here in this garden. With Us, here in you, you truly live."

The more the words flowed from His mouth, the more the beauty around her grew. She believed, she really believed, that His life was now her life.

"Guard the truth in you now." He caught her attention, because she realized she still had a part to play in this flourishing life.

"Stop allowing yourself to be agitated by others, and stay in the Spirit. Remain in Me. Keep your mind here. When it starts to stray or think negatively or complain, bring it back here to this land. There is life here. You need to live as if you are free, because you are."

She again realized her great need of His continued wisdom and revelation, even on this side of the river, and asked, "How do I stop being agitated?" She knew this was one of her greatest adversaries.

"The Holy Spirit will remind you of all you have learned here so that you can live in this flourishing state of your garden all the time."

She continued to watch life flourish around her.

"That's why I gave you the memorial stones. Get them back out and spend time with Me in the secret place, for I will strengthen you there. Meditate on Me, for I am the only one who can keep you in that undisturbed place."

She felt great peace flood her soul as she listened with her whole heart.

"And when you are teaching others, teach them to go all the way into the Promised Land, not just halfway. Tell them not to settle for half the promise. In other words, tell them they must not settle for half the weeds remaining in their gardens, saying of themselves, 'Oh well, the rest of my garden looks okay.' No, convince them that the weeds remaining will multiply and try to take over their whole garden life."

She thought about a verse she had recently read in her Bible about Abraham, who was at the time called Abram because God had not yet given him his new name. It said of him that on the way to the Promised Land, that he came to Haran and settled there.

Zoe asked Jesus, "Haran was halfway to the Promised Land, wasn't it?"

He loved the wisdom that continued growing in her.

"Yes, it was. Circumstances, situations, the Enemy, and even your own thoughts always try to talk you out of what God has said and done in you. Just like in the garden of Eden at the beginning of the Bible, where the serpent came into the garden and said, 'Did God really say not to eat the fruit of this tree?' or maybe now asks, 'Do you really think you are healed of your past?' He'll even say things like 'You are not good enough' or 'Every time you open your mouth you sound stupid' or 'You need to do this or that first, before you can ever do anything for God, before you can hand someone some of your fruit.' The Enemy will always lie to you, because that is who he is."

Zoe felt His fruitfulness filling her soul.

Jesus continued, "Don't just go halfway into the fullness and fruitfulness God has for your soul. Cross all the way into the things that I have promised you. Tell others what took place in you today, and then tell them to cross their Jordan and to go into their Promised Land. You need to hold on to the promises I have given to you and tell others to cling to their promises also."

She thought about all the half-truths she had once believed about herself.

"The whole world, including a lot of Christians, is stuck, Zoe. People are stuck halfway into the Promised Land. Convince them to cross over like you have today and then to give out the life and the fruit that they have received. That's also what I desire from you, Zoe: to give what you have been given by spending intimate time with Me, your Maker. Then the ones you touch can become a flourishing garden too, able to hand out life-giving fruit, which is nourishment to others."

Zoe smiled widely and said, "You have given me the key to this life of nourishing others; I now know it to be intimacy with You. Time spent with You is the key to this flourishing garden life."

Jesus smiled in return and replied, "In the garden things are constant. I am constant in every circumstance. Most people respond in the flesh to the situations and circumstances surrounding them. I want you to respond in the Spirit, with Me holding your every thought and action. Let's see. Let Me give you an example."

Zoe loved the way He always knew how to word things so that she would grasp the truth He was revealing.

"It is like the difference between a thermometer and a thermostat. Thermometers go up and down depending on the weather—or the situation, in this instance. That is like the flesh, which says 'I'm up' or 'I'm down' and is always changing. But a thermostat is different: you set it and it stays there, and it has the ability to change a room's temperature. That is walking in My Spirit—setting your mind on me constantly, and responding with Me in your thoughts and actions. So when you walk into a room or a situation, conscious of Me walking with and in you; that alone has the ability to change the atmosphere of that room or situation."

Zoe loved that even in the Promised Land, He continued to teach her. She loved to be taught by the Lord.

"So, Zoe, when your flesh starts to rule and you feel it changing the temperature of peace, encourage yourself in the Lord your God. Speak to your soul, tell it to be quiet, and set your every thought on Me. Take a peace break. Walk away from the situation for a moment, and focus on My plan for it. I always have a plan." He grinned. "Come to the garden, remind Me of My promises, and remind yourself what I have said to you. And when discouragement and depression start, right then pray. Talk to Me, and then listen. Let My peace rule as an umpire in your heart continuously."

Zoe visualized her Jesus in a baseball umpire suit and giggled.

He said, "Yep, that's My job." He made the "safe" gesture, as an umpire would make with a runner sliding into a base. "I call you safe," He said.

And she felt safe in Him.

He said, "The Enemy sometimes makes halfway feel comfortable. It's like when you get used to the cold if you've been in it awhile. He does this to keep you from going all the way into fullness and fruitfulness, and he will make you comfortable where you are." He placed one hand on His chest and His other on hers. "Enter all the way into all that I have promised and said of you. Believe and cling to them and to Me. You have the ability to change the world, because I am walking in it with you."

Zoe hated the cold; she had no desire to stay there physically or spiritually.

"Stay completely within the fullness of what I have for you; it's in the crossing that you give out the abundant life. Work with and for Me, and give what you've been given. Plant in others and water others, and I will make them grow."

As He said this, all of a sudden something appeared before them that looked like a scroll, and as it rolled open they were looking at the earth from a different place.

Could this be the view from heaven? she thought. She could see the earth revolving and was astounded by the scene before her.

"The whole earth is groaning, wanting the children of the living God to arise." He placed His hand on the side of her head, and they were face-to-face. "Arise now, Zoe, My life giver, and shine. Pour forth and give life to those I have appointed you to; give My life. They are waiting. Some may not know it yet, but they are waiting."

He reassured her with a smile. "My words are nourishment, and people could die without the nourishment or truth that you have in you. I have qualified you to tell others of My goodness and to make My life available to them. Teach, admonish, and train. I need you. Others need you, and you need others. Encourage one another in Me."

He looked out into the sky and seemed to make a star shine brighter just with a glance. "In teaching you will learn, and in learning you will teach."

Zoe was so captivated, not only by Him, but also by the view before her eyes. "The universe declares Your glory," she said with a quiver in her voice as she continued to gaze down at the world and across the universe.

"I just want you to know something," He said.

Her gaze returned to Him.

"There is no responsibility on you for this work; the only responsibility you have is to keep in living, constant touch with Me and to not allow anything at all to hinder your cooperation with Me."

His voice was filled with more compassion than she had ever heard in Him as He spoke directly into her soul.

"The things that used to keep your life pinned down are gone. They are gone, Zoe."

Tears once again flowed from her eyes.

"You are free for one purpose only: to be absolutely devoted to Me and to share Me with those around you. Take hold of My strength, the strength that I provide, and completely surrender to My protection. I pray that My roots will go down deep inside of you and that you will blossom, send forth shoots, and fill the whole world with the knowledge of the one true God, of Me."

Zoe looked back to the earth, and they were instantly back in her garden, back to the first place where she entered into her soul with Jesus by her side. The garden that had once looked so dead was now filled with life, blossoms, color, and vibrancy. She hardly recognized the place and could not believe the change.

The Garden Within

She was standing on the path where she first saw the signs of life inside of her and said, "You know, Jesus, when we first came here, this path was covered with thistles and thorns, but just look what You have done! You have caused my garden to flourish and to be fruitful." She continued looking around, and then she looked back at Him. "I love to be here with You, and I will come here every day. You made it alive again; you made me live again." She took in a deep breath. So thankful. So alive.

Jesus smiled and placed Zoe's last stone, a round one, in her palm.

"It looks like the earth," she said, and she smiled.

"When you find Me in your heart, you will find Me everywhere. Your garden is alive now. It's alive and awake. And if you look outside of it and gaze with My eyes, you will see that the whole world is a garden."

At that last statement, Zoe was standing in her physical garden at home. She looked out into her world and smiled.

The end—or, actually, just the beginning.

But thanks be to God, Who in Christ always leads us in triumph, as trophies of Christ's victory, and through us spreads and makes evident the fragrance of the knowledge of God everywhere.
2 Corinthians 2:14

Behold the days are coming, says the Lord, that everything heretofore barren and unfruitful shall overflow with spiritual blessing.
Amos 9:13

In the whole world [the Gospel] is bearing fruit and still is growing.
Colossians 1:6

The gardens around me are blooming now.
Zoe

Scripture References

The Lord sat with me as I wrote this book, which came from studying the Scriptures and going through previous journals with Him. In the book I used *pieces or ideas* from all of the following Scriptures which were taken from the *Amplified Bible*. *Grand Rapids:* Zondervan, 1987. After reading the book, I encourage you to look up the Scripture references listed here and ask Jesus for more revelation. For more encouragement or to contact me, you can visit my website: www.gardenwithinministries.com

Chapter 1~The Garden

- » John 10:7
- » Song of Solomon 1:3
- » Psalm 119:103
- » Song of Solomon 4:12
- » Song of Solomon 2:10
- » Song of Solomon 1:6
- » Jeremiah 1:5

- » Hebrews 12:2
- » Song of Solomon 2:10
- » Song of Solomon 2:14

Chapter 2~A Secret Process

- » Ecclesiastes 3:1
- » Hosea 10:12
- » Genesis 50:20
- » Hosea 2:15
- » Isaiah 27:6
- » Song of Solomon 5:1–2

Chapter 3~Awakened

- » Song of Solomon 5:16
- » Song of Solomon 1:15
- » Song of Solomon 4:12
- » Joel 2:25
- » 2 Kings 8:6
- » Song of Solomon 2:3
- » Song of Solomon 2:6

Chapter 4~Dark But Comely

- » 1. Song of Solomon 1, footnotes in *Amplified Bible. Grand Rapids:* Zondervan, 1987 p.966-967 *slightly adapted*
- » 2. Amazing grace; written by John Newton
- » Psalm 56:8
- » Ezekiel 36:35
- » Joshua 4

Chapter 5~Foundation

» Ephesians 4:29
» Proverbs 18:21
» Psalm 19:14

Chapter 6~Purpose

» Jeremiah 31:3
» Psalm 91:1
» Song of Solomon 8:14
» Song of Solomon 7:1
» Song of Solomon 6:1

Chapter 7~Life

» Hebrews 12:11
» 1. Bickersteth, *Streams in the Desert*, Mrs. Charles E. Cowman (Grand Rapids: Zondervan, pg.193), .
» Ezekiel 36:26
» Matthew 15:13
» Matthew 12:34

Chapter 8~The Vineyard

» 1. God has a purpose in view. Often we shrink from the purging and pruning, forgetting the Gardener knows, that the deeper the cutting and paring, the richer the luster that grows.- *Streams in the Desert*, Mrs. Charles E. Cowman (Grand Rapids: Zondervan August 9, pg. 249)
» Romans 8:28
» Genesis 41:52
» Matthew 28:18–20

- » Isaiah 27:2–6
- » Isaiah 61:3

Chapter 9~Come For A Swim

- » John 14:26
- » Song of Solomon 2:8
- » John 7:38
- » 1 John 2:16
- » Isaiah 58:11
- » Jeremiah 17:8
- » John 16:33
- » Isaiah 12:3
- » Proverbs 18:4
- » Ezekiel 47:9
- » Isaiah 35:1
- » Isaiah 41:18

Chapter 10~Weeds

- » Isaiah 26:14
- » Matthew 13:25
- » 1. The Message Remix

Chapter 11~Under The Cedar Tree

- » Colossians 3:2
- » 1 Peter 5:9
- » Proverbs 24:30–32
- » Jeremiah 17: 6–7

Chapter 12~You Look Just Like Your Dad

- » Jeremiah 18: 1–6

- » Isaiah 45:9
- » Isaiah 64:8
- » Genesis 1:26
- » 2 Corinthians 4:7

Chapter 13~I Will Change Your Name

- » Isaiah 62:2
- » John 1:42
- » Luke 6:14
- » Genesis 32:24–30
- » Genesis 17:5,15
- » Numbers 13:16
- » Acts 13:9
- » Acts 4:36
- » Acts 15:22
- » Matthew 10:13
- » Acts 12:25
- » Acts 15:37
- » Joel 2:25

Chapter 14~Fruit

- » John 17:3
- » Genesis 1:28
- » Galatians 5:22
- » John 15
- » Genesis 41:52
- » Isaiah 26:3–6
- » Hosea 14:8

Chapter 15~Crossing The Jordon

- » John 14:27

- » Colossians 3:15
- » 2 Corinthians 3:6
- » Colossians 3:14–17
- » Isaiah 27:6

Sources

Amplified Bible. Grand Rapids: Zondervan, 1987.

Streams in the Desert. Grand Rapids: Zondervan.

The Message Remix. Eugene H. Peterson: Navpress

Made in the USA
Monee, IL
09 December 2021